Financial Strategy in the Acquisition Decision

Financial Strategy in the Acquisition Decision

D G Bean

Gower Press

First published in Great Britain by
Gower Press Limited 1975

Reprinted 1978 by
Gower Press, Teakfield Limited,
Westmead, Farnborough, Hants., England

Reprinted 1979

ISBN 0 7161 0268 4

Printed in Great Britain by
Biddles Ltd, Guildford, Surrey

Contents

Illustrations

Figure

Figure

Preface

The general literature concerning mergers and acquisitions amongst companies can broadly be classified into the academic and the managerial, mostly prescriptive, literature. There appears to be relatively little attempt in any of these bodies of knowledge to match the content to the area of practice. The fact that there are many different theories concerning merger incidence and a rich body of managerial literature suggests that different parts of the literature relate to different areas of observed practice. In particular the highly publicized 'asset-stripping' activity of certain UK quoted public companies appears to bear little relationship to accepted economic ideas of mergers designed to reap economies of scale, vertical integration benefits or super-profits from monopolization.

The focus of this study is upon financial activity in acquisitions; in particular it attempts to distinguish from companies which engage in acquisition and merger the existence, aims and operating procedures of certain types of 'financially-oriented' companies that pursue growth mainly by acquisition. The behaviour of this group of companies was examined by means of interviews and case studies. The original research and results formed the basis for a PhD dissertation at Manchester Business School. This book integrates the main findings of my thesis together with other aspects of the theory and empirical evidence of business finance with a view to providing a discussion of acquisition activity that connects with literature concerning share price movements and portfolio theory.

Appreciation of the nature of speculative market price movements is important for understanding both the nature of risk in financial markets and consequently the practical realizations of portfolio concepts. In addition the valuation of financial instruments such as warrants and convertible loans as well as ordinary shares reflects the nature of speculative market price movements. Following introductory comments in Chapter 1, Chapter 2 introduces random walk concepts regarding speculative market price movements and then discusses portfolio theory implications for acquisition analysis and strategy.

The fact that business is conducted under conditions of risk and uncertainty suggests that in practice decision-makers form rules of thumb for guidance and that some of these rules of thumb ultimately become widely accepted. Banking security ratios are a case in point. Chapter 3 discusses certain rules of thumb which are concerned with acquisition financing and formulates them into testable propositions.

Chapter 4 discusses aspects of acquisition bargaining between seller or 'target' company and the acquirer. The distribution of target company shareholdings, degree of asset backing and type of acquisition financing package are considered as interrelated aspects of the bargaining process. The selection of financing instruments is discussed with reference to the nature of share price movements and duration of deferred equity rights.

Chapter 5 is concerned with methods of search and evaluation for possible acquisition target companies. Models are formed as tentative descriptions of search and evaluation processes. These models are primarily concerned with financial aspects of acquisitions but could be extended to handle non-financial acquisition criteria. Chapter 6 summarizes the main concepts of the book.

Whilst referring to underlying academic papers and texts, the book is concerned to avoid much quantitative argument and rather discusses concepts in a qualitative manner. Results from my thesis are presented where empirical research was carried out relevant to the topic of discussion. These results tended to be on small samples and readers may treat the empirical evidence with circumspection. The material presented in this book aims to strike a balance between theoretical arguments and their practical implications. It is intended that executives and corporate planners in commerce and industry will find a theoretical framework against which to refer ideas of corporate acquisition activity whilst students of business finance and corporate strategy may link theoretical concepts to practice by way of the case examples contained in the text. Essentially the book is aimed towards businessmen concerned with corporate strategy and planning and towards postgraduate students in business administration.

I would particularly like to acknowledge the help and guidance I received during the course of my thesis from Professors E.A. Lowe and G.H. Lawson. In addition many former colleagues at Manchester Business School assisted me in connection with my thesis and amongst them were Derek Channon, Bryan Elliott, Robert Fildes, Morris McInnes and Gerald Newbould, to all of whom I owe thanks as well as to colleagues on the doctoral programme. I of course take full responsibility for the opinions expressed in this book and for remaining defects and errors.

I would also like to thank Mrs J. Scholes and Mrs J. Scammells for typing many drafts of my thesis so patiently and proficiently.

Although I cannot name individuals whom I interviewed in the course of my thesis, I wish to thank all of them most sincerely for the time that they, as busy top executives, were able to give me. I hope that in summarizing opinions I have faithfully reproduced and integrated their comments.

The support of the Ford Foundation and that of the Foundation for Management Education for funding of the doctoral programme at Manchester Business School is gratefully acknowledged.

Finally I would like to thank my parents for their generosity during the earlier part of my education.

D G Bean

1

Financial Factors in Acquisition Analysis

Introduction

Of all the strategic decisions which business executives make few have such speedy repercussions as acquisition investments. Whatever the underlying motives for a deal may be, it is the financial details which tend to be subjected to the most immediate scrutiny and the most objective assessment. The quality of acquisition decisions made by publicly quoted companies is reflected in their stock market capitalizations; in the case of private companies carefully conceived financing plans for a deal are an important factor in raising the required funds. Even if the overall advantages of an acquisition are soundly assessed, failure to produce a financing plan which is attractive to financial institutions and investors over the medium term of up to three years can have severe consequences upon the capitalization of a company and its future financing ability. Therefore analysis of financial objectives and influences in acquisition decisions is of paramount importance to a policy of external growth.

Most acquisition activity is cast as an aggressive form of expansion for the acquirer company; however the discussion will be equally applicable to defensive acquisitions where the objective is not concerned with economic expansion but rather prevention of decline. Indeed the increasing concern about continued economic growth in the world and more specifically in Western economies may defuse the current macro-economic preoccupations with growth. Reduced economic growth for a time may stress the quality aspects of an economy rather than its quantity of output. In this event it is likely that combination and deployment of resources – manpower, materials and capital goods – will all change significantly. Thus the need for an adaptive approach to corporate development becomes important and, if one agrees that change is the one certainty facing executives, then both aggressive and defensive categories of acquisition activity are unlikely to diminish. For similar reasons one may expect the increasing trade in divisions of larger corporations to continue. Even lack of overall growth in an economy does not preclude growth-seeking behaviour at the micro-economic level of the individual firm although the possibilities are reduced. Instead it implies a tightening control on the use of resources and, in a moderately competitive capitalist economy, greater financial efficiency. Consequently capital investment decisions, both internal and external by way of acquisition, are likely to remain a crucial part of corporate development planning but with a more defensive viewpoint which stresses sophistication in resource combination and utilization coupled with effort to insulate from product market vulnerabilities.

Development of a firm by acquisition investment may indeed offer a swift means of implementing change and promoting shareholder wealth, but it is not without hazards. One of a number of lessons which the US conglomerate era in the 1960s provided was that financial ties alone between companies are not sufficient to produce a vehicle for developing shareholder wealth once acquisition activity slows down. To regard a firm solely as a financial system ignores the richness of organization, production facilities, manpower, contacts external to the firm and specialist operating experience of its employees, all of which and more combine to create a viable operating system. For a firm to function at all there has to be some balance between the various resources of manpower, machinery, materials and finance and the demand for services from the firm. Accounting concepts of stocks and flows have wider implications than purely financial statement analysis and, even if measurement in value terms is difficult, provide concepts which help to identify sources of value in a firm beyond its balance sheet. For example labour skills, technical excellence and good labour relations are stores of value in a firm which are relevant to a potential acquirer company but are not directly reflected in financial statements It can be argued that such attributes are reflected in stock market rating or in financial results such as turnover per employee; however it is difficult to prove this in view of the complexity of the economic systems concerned. Ideally in an acquisition, or for that matter the disposal of a business, the benefits are gained from creating a better balance of resource utilization and product market positions than existed before the deal. Hazards arise when the overall vision of a business combination hides serious imbalances or disorganization in underlying operating systems of the combining companies. Although the arguments of this book are couched in financial terms this is largely because finance provides the most comprehensive common language between the underlying 'physical' operating components of a firm. Not being a perfectly comprehensive language, financial theory can provide only partial models of business enterprise.

One of the main concepts in financial theory and in the theory of the firm is that the firm is operated to maximize the net present value of the wealth of its shareholders. Much research into business behaviour shows that firms do not pursue such single-minded capitalistic objectives. In particular managers perform a certain amount of featherbedding for themselves by way of fringe benefits and expense allowances; departmental rivalries and desire for personal promotion lead managers to invest in projects which in truth may not have justifiable commercial returns for shareholders; advertising may be set at a fixed percentage of turnover rather than on a commercial basis; acquisitions may be made to expand turnover at the expense of earnings and assets per share; excess staff may be built up when business is booming. Although many areas can be cited in which actual behaviour deviates from the idealized shareholder net present wealth maximization model, such deviations do not invalidate that model but rather act as constraints upon its region of feasibility. A non-controlling shareholder can rationalize the point by arguing that it is necessary to give up a certain amount of the potential maximal returns to obtain a functioning business enterprise. However, a member of the whole body of shareholders has the power of sanctioning management and ultimately of dismissal. Certainly in the US and increasingly so in the UK this shareholder power can be put to work, even if it is employed surreptitiously behind the scenes. Management may not only be deterred from excessive concern with their own ends by the threat of shareholder voting power but much more likely by takeover vulnerability, as Marris (1966) has argued. Consequently the concept of shareholder net present wealth maximization is not only constrained on the upside by managerial self-fulfilment but also on the downside by stock market and legal sanctions. Furthermore the impact of risks and uncertainties in the business environment will normally preclude maximization of the net present value of a company in any meaningful sense. However, none of these qualifications prevent the firm from retaining a conceptual but realistically weak objective of maximizing the net present wealth of shareholders subject to constraints which remain for the present unspecified in an environment which contains risks and uncertainties. To translate this concept into more meaningful terms for acquisition strategy requires deeper consideration of the main influences on the capitalization of a company as a result of acquisition decisions and discussion of strategies for operation under conditions of risk. Although many of the problems which come to light from these discussions have been the subject of considerable mathematical and statistical consideration, the aim of the book is to present and integrate ideas in a largely non-mathematical form.

The firm as an operating system – implications for financial analysis

Research into facets of business enterprise has proceeded from many directions and disciplines ranging from micro-economics and finance to organizational sociology and industrial psychology. No single discipline can pretend to explain the overall operation of a firm nor has any general theory of the firm been proposed which adequately combines the approaches of all the various disciplines. Courageous attempts to integrate small parts of the knowledge gained from these various research approaches have been made. Notable amongst them is the work of Forrester (1961) in his 'industrial dynamics' approach to quantitative models of the firm which attempts to provide a model system with self-control mechanisms. Although many firms have built forecasting and representational models, an example being the BP 'Firm' model based on a linear programming specification, creation of adaptive models of business enterprise is still in its infancy. Nor is this surprising when the complexity of internal and external operations and relationships, even for a small firm, is considered. But from an overall decision-making viewpoint it is necessary to abstract and cut away some of the fine mesh of interrelationships to reveal what are thought to be the more important factors. Thus it is apparent that there are deeper bodies of knowledge about particular aspects of business operation from particular viewpoints, for example organizational theory from a sociological viewpoint or labour relations from that of the industrial psychologist, but there is relatively little theory about the firm as a whole which integrates the main parts of each component body. Most of the integrated theory is economic or financial in orientation, not least perhaps because financial data is the easiest to obtain. The point to be made therefore is that although it is recognized that the firm is an entity of complex components neither the theory nor data at present available allow it to be analysed as such in any non-controversial or prescribed way. The best that can be done is to use the available quantitative, largely financial data and, being aware of its limitations as to comprehensiveness and reporting limitations etc, interpret it, together with whatever qualitative information is regarded as relevant. Most companies which engage seriously in acquisitions eventually build up procedures for data gathering and check lists for analysis which facilitate this process.

It is relevant to indicate some of the major connections between financing, investment and marketing decisions which face business executives since a material acquisition is an act which has direct ramifications in all three component operating systems of a company. Internal capital investments, unless accompanied by substantial and sudden changes in financing of the firm, will generally not have immediate financing repercussions and will tend in most cases not to produce sudden shifts in product market dependence since build-up to full operations is progressive. Whereas the familiar discounted cash flow capital budgeting model, given for the present the assumption of adequate and correct information about the future, provides a straightforward basis for internal capital investment appraisals, there are a number of complicating problems in extending it to cope with acquisitions. For example if financial markets adjust the rating of the acquirer company shares in response to the acquisition then the implied cost of capital to the company alters. To this end it may be asked whether the riskiness of the acquirer company's earnings is likely to alter as a result of the acquisition and thereby affect the company's share price rating; also whether the rating is likely to be affected by the choice of financing package, ie the mixture of cash, loans and equity employed. Looking deeper into the acquisition it may be questioned whether the riskiness of the acquired firm's earnings is likely to be affected by labour relations or union problems arising from the combination of the companies. In the latter instance there is a movement away from readily quantifiable factors into more qualitative judgmental areas which signify the need for further information specific to the particular problem.

Limitations of optimization techniques. Typically an acquisition analysis comprises both qualitative and quantitative information which may be gained from many sources. The qualitative information may be seen as backing up the quantitative assessments and as a means of reducing uncertainty about particular aspects of the acquisition. But the question has also been posed as to how the quantitative measures should be evaluated once their values are specified. There are difficulties in using a discounted cash flow model resulting from the link between financing and investment decisions. In addition the choice of investment horizon for capital budgeting projections of returns is not a simple one where a company is changing rapidly and has an opportunistic approach to its future development. Too long a horizon will involve forecasting of events which are very likely to be altered in the process of change and by external events, whereas too short a horizon may ignore many of the longer-term attractions of the acquisition. Concepts of simultaneous optimization over investment, financing and product market operations of the firm can only apply realistically for the very few firms with relatively stable circumstances not subject to external pressures on their fortunes. Until late 1973 the example might have been cited of an oil-refining and distributing firm as one for which relatively stable operating circumstances provided a suitable environment for optimization techniques in overall planning. The BP 'Firm' model based upon linear programming was a case in point. The dramatic changes arising from the use of monopoly power by oil exporters provides a sharp lesson in the need for flexibility in corporate planning and its implementation.

The complexity of the internal operating systems of a firm has been touched upon but of greater significance is the fact that each firm is uniquely embedded into its external environment especially by economic and social ties. Relationships with suppliers and customers are not between automata but between people; not without just reason is 'goodwill' frequently mentioned particularly in connection with professional practices. Biological analogues of firms have been advanced for the corporation system as in Beer's *The Brain of the Firm* (1972); Beer's stimulating ideas have not received implementation upon which assessment of their practical significance can be made. The problems of creating workable models of 'open systems', namely systems which are not largely self-sufficient but rely upon exchange of influences across their boundaries, in the economic and financial areas have become most developed in the case of econometric models. Even if allowance is made for statistical difficulties in estimation, their success in representation of open systems for predictive purposes has been questionable. In summary the problem is that frequently descriptive models can be built which apply well to projections of existing corporate circumstances and structures but, as one might expect, fail to cope with an adaptive environment and fail to assist non-repetitive management decisions.

Behavioural approach. It has been argued more extensively elsewhere[1] that in adaptive environments, such as the economic, social and political circumstances surrounding corporate operations, managers pursue 'satisficing' behaviour. That is to say they seek good achievable solutions to problems rather than attempts at optimal solutions over wide-ranging decisions. For example, rather than try to optimize an acquisition selection on all components of product market, investment and financing with full information about all possible acquisition candidates, the search is narrowed down progressively by consideration of a certain size of company, restricted to certain industries, and to those firms with widespread shareholdings. Within such criteria an acquisition target is selected and then attempts are made to find the best financing plan. Therefore instead of considering the niceties of overall optimization the problem has been vastly narrowed by a search sequence which, as Cyert and March (1963) suggest in their book *A Behavioural Theory of the Firm*, may be characterized in terms of goals, sub-goals, aspiration levels towards the goals and use of operating rules to achieve such goals. When aspiration levels are not achieved then they may be reduced or if they fall too low then the problem may be abandoned.

Explanation of business activity from a behavioural viewpoint is therefore much more concerned with integrating ideas about the functioning of individuals within the organizational structure of a firm and with the effects of motivations and constraints upon people rather than the explanation of business activity purely in terms of aggregated economic theories of the firm. Behavioural theory is also concerned with decision-making in response to incomplete and uncertain information about the future, which generally implies that a formalized (mathematical) structure of the decision is likely to be difficult if not impossible to solve optimally given the present state of techniques such as programming, simulation etc.

In favouring the current leaning towards behavioural explanations of business behaviour it is reasonable to ask whether optimization techniques have any role within planning for adaptive future circumstances. The foregoing discussion has argued that optimization techniques are only applicable to circumstances where all the decision variables, influences, structure and consequences of a problem can be defined. For example, although the overall operations of many oil companies have been seriously altered by the exceptional use of monopoly power by oil-exporting countries, the operations of an oil refinery are not altered and the analytic methods used in their production control remain appropriate although the output objectives of refinery product mix may have changed. Sophisticated analytic techniques can be of great assistance to executives provided they are used in their appropriate places where their assumptions are adequately satisfied. Financial strategy in acquisition decisions, which are almost invariably made in circumstances of incomplete knowledge, and for which change is frequently an important objective, will be considered broadly in 'satisficing' terms but with certain aspects which are amenable to optimizing treatments.

Valuation of companies with reference to financial market price movements

The interrelated aspects of investment and financing decisions through financial market forces have been noted already. Valuation of a company for acquisition is a complex problem in which influences external as well as internal to the combining companies, referred to as acquirer and target companies respectively, are significant. The most important external influence is that arising from overall movements in the stock market and in interest rates. Valuation of publicly quoted companies is directly linked to equity market price movements whereas valuation of private companies may be expected to link more closely with movements in fixed interest stocks and overdraft interest rates due to the greater funding reliance of private companies upon banking sources. In general therefore the timing of acquisitions from both buyer's and seller's viewpoints should pay considerable attention to equity and fixed interest market movements.

Capital budgeting approach. It has been argued that, although a company may be valued by reference to its instantaneous share price, a more relevant measure is given by adopting a capital budgeting approach to expected future dividend flows available to ordinary shareholders. Conversely it can also be argued that the value of a share or of a company is merely the value in exchange between willing buyers and willing sellers and is therefore equal to the value quoted in the stock market. The capital budgeting approach has been labelled 'intrinsic' worth valuation as if the instantaneous stock market valuation represents intrinsic worth together with some error component which may be positive or negative depending upon whether overall market capitalization of the company's equity exceeds or falls short of intrinsic worth. A treatment of this approach may be found in the collection of papers on acquisition valuation edited by Alberts and Segall (1966); the papers by Weston and by Alberts are of particular relevance. If the capital budgeting argument is extended to the point of saying that on a discounted cash flow model the expected future dividend flows to shareholders imply a valuation of £X/share (avoiding for the present the problem of determining a discount rate) and the shares sell at £Y on the market, it can be appreciated how the multitude of valuations made by individual investors creates a market with fluctuating prices for a company's shares. Although perhaps only a small number of market participants adopt a formal capital budgeting model approach to share valuation, it seems reasonable to assume that all investors use information to form their best judgment about the future for the share in which they are interested.

A pure value-in-exchange viewpoint of share valuation recognizes the opportunity cost nature of a shareholder's investment in that at certain times his utility for investment in stocks and shares is high and at other times low. Personal as well as overall economic circumstances impinge on the utilities of investors. Any perceived discrepancy of a capital budgeting approach to corporate valuation versus that of a value-in-exchange approach is possibly more a matter of definition of the discount rate which is employed in the capital budgeting valuation model. The discount rate for a particular investor is essentially a subjective and personal matter derived from utility considerations for deferral of consumption by way of investment.

Stock market price movements. A wealth of research has been conducted into the nature of stock market price movements, in particular to ask whether the price of a share today yields any help in prediction of its price tomorrow. Most of this research is of a statistical nature and can be broadly described under the argument that price changes over equal periods in stock markets are random and can be categorized in a particular statistical distributional form (stable non-normal). Broadly this means that a knowledge of historical price changes alone does not help in making future share trading profits. Linked with the idea that prices move randomly is the argument that new information reaching the market is discounted very quickly into share prices so that investors can only profit from inside information and not from acting on generally available information. Intuitively there would be a tendency to agree with this result in that a large number of existing and potential investors in a firm, if given the same information about the firm's future, would tend to form share valuations distributed around some figure (the average) and in trading upon their expectations would cause prices to fluctuate in a statistical sense around that average value. However there would be no reason for any trend movement about the average unless new and more optimistic/pessimistic information was constantly becoming available which caused investors to progressively upgrade/downgrade their valuation estimates. More extensive reference to the underlying research and arguments may be found in a survey paper by Fama (1970).

If stock market prices move randomly it is reasonable to question why there appear to be quite well-defined cycles in stock markets of duration between three and five years but of varying volatility. Can apparent cycles and trends so much beloved by chartist followers be at all consistent with the extensive research which supports random price movements? At first sight the answer is no but further analysis suggests that there may be some overlap. The author's own research on random walks in speculative market price movements suggests that there may be 'non-stationarity' in the parameters of price movement distributions, in other words that the distributions of, say, daily price changes do not remain exactly the same over a period of time but change to some extent both in volatility and in trend. However one must recognize that any measures of price movements, whether they be in statistical terms or graphically illustrated on charts, only concern a particular time span. The interest lies in whether one can predict what the next time span will be like. So far no model, be it a chartist, econometric, or pure statistical forecasting method, has been able to predict stock market price movements over more than a couple of years. Again this should not be surprising since the stock market is an open system *par excellence* where response to unexpected external events is the rule rather than the exception. Consequently creation of models for the purpose of predicting share prices which are based on the past history of an economy are unlikely to be of great use unless the future can be assumed not to introduce fresh and unexpected circumstances. Indeed, if one generates a sequence of random price movements consistent with past price distributions, it is quite surprising how closely a chart of the generated sequence illustrates apparent trends and cycles. At a more academic level, if the distribution of price movements in speculative markets is well approximated by the stable non-normal form then many of the existing statistical methods of analysis for identification of cycles become strictly invalidated. For further reading in this fascinating area reference should be made to the work of Mandelbrot (1963) and (1969) and to that of Granger and Morgenstern (1970).

Many professional investors and those close to stock markets would argue that investor psychology, although difficult to quantify, is a concept helpful in understanding the market and that experience of trading enables one to assess market turning points with reasonable accuracy. In the author's view the random walk theory results still leave some room for predictable behaviour in the longer-term movements of markets, which in statistical terms may become apparent from non-stationarity of parameters that define the distributions of short-term price movement sequences. In fact a certain amount of common ground may exist between some chartist concepts and these longer-term movements but much more research would be required to investigate this idea. For the purposes of this book the viewpoint is adopted that speculative market price movements including equities, fixed-interest company securities and gilts are largely random in the short term of up to probably one year. Beyond that there may be aspects of price movements which allow prediction, most important of which for acquisition analysis would be the ability to assess major market turning points which have been apparent at between three- to five-year intervals.

Financial market approval of acquisition decisions

The preceding discussion has implied that largely random movements of prices can explain the apparent cycles and trends in security markets. A further implication associated with random price movements is that financial markets are near perfect in the accepted sense of having many participants none of whom hold excessive market power and all of whom have access to the same information. In these market circumstances if in addition there were no costs of transactions such as brokerage fees and stamp duties, nor taxes, either on companies or on traders in securities, one would expect that the overall cost of capital to a company would be the same whatever its component proportions of fixed-interest debt and equity capital. This is the argument first propounded by Modigliani and Miller (1958). However, subsequent discussion and research has reached the general consensus of opinion that transaction costs and differential tax rates on debt and equity finance make debt preferable to equity as a source of finance up to some point in a firm's capital structure. If too much debt is incurred then the equity valuation of the firm will tend to decline to more than offset the advantage of higher debt and its consequent tax-deductible interest charges.

For acquisition-financing decisions it is important to aim at a good capital structure for the combined operations. Indeed acquisitions provide means of improving capital structure of an under- or over-geared company. A review of loan stock instrument terms indicates that financial institutions seek to limit the amount of loan interest in relation to pre-tax profits and keep an adequate amount of net tangible asset backing to cover loan principal. These are examples of rule-of-thumb methods which aim to keep a company's financial structure within limits approved by investors.

It will be argued that further financial limitations exist upon acquisition selection and financing. These concern first the maximum size of an acquisition relative to the acquirer company's capitalization, second the effects of the acquisition upon earnings per share of the acquirer company before and after the deal, and third the effect upon asset backing per share of the acquirer. Together with loan stock capital structure limitations these may be visualized as constraints upon feasible acquisitions that will not damage the investment standing of the acquirer company. In association with the conceptual objective of acquisitions, namely to maximize shareholder net present wealth, they indicate a means of formulating financing packages for acquisitions in a scientific manner which is more fully described in Chapter 3. On this view, the capitalization of a firm which achieves positive gains in assets or earnings per share as a result of an acquisition that also fulfils the size and loan stock cover constraints should rise and thereby benefit its shareholders.

Sequences of such acquisitions provide a mechanism of wealth creation by acquisition in some respects analogous to the US conglomerate era in the 1960s, although the conglomerates mostly failed to keep asset and earnings per share growth in step with each other. Although the US conglomerates failed partly from the accounting opportunities by which they were able to delude investors and partly from failure to create realized gains which provided a solid asset backing increment to share prices, acquisition-minded UK companies have until recently been much more successful in maintaining growth in shareholders' wealth from primarily acquisition-based expansion policies. Notable amongst these companies were some of the satellite companies of Slater Walker and Jessel Securities which grew quickly by acquisition during the early 1970s.

Gains from acquisition – problems of risk and uncertainty assessment

The distinction between assets and earnings in accounting terms, with which investors are familiar from reading financial statements of companies, is largely a red herring which has grown up with the increasingly diverse and incompatible objectives which published financial statements attempt to reconcile. That one set of financial statements should with only minor modifications attempt to provide a basis for legal reporting requirements, investor information, tax calculations and political disclosures is the more amazing as the reporting complexities of each requirement expand with time. The needs of investors are largely related to cash measures of company profitability and survival, namely solvency, liquidity, realizability, funds available for investment and dividend flows. Such measures as accrued earnings per share, accrued assets per share and loan stock covers from accrued earnings and accrued assets are but proxies for the important measures associated with cash flows and realizable cash stocks. Acquirer company executives do need to be hard-nosed about the cash equivalence and realizability of assets and earnings stated in accrued accounting terms. In acquisition activity there can be a world of difference between accrued accounting and cash flow valuations of business enterprises. The latter is the correct one with which to be concerned.

Difficulties associated with capital budgeting. A cash flow outlook to enterprise valuation brings one back to the capital budgeting discounted cash flow model of valuation, some of the practical difficulties of which have already been mentioned. Strictly the capital budgeting model examines future cash flows to an infinite horizon point. For practical purposes the impact of uncertainties in the sense of unknowable events makes nonsense of long-term perspectives for most business enterprise. The temptation to reject capital budgeting methods on this account however should be resisted since it confuses the problem of quantification with the problem of finding a conceptually correct valuation method. Constructively one needs to find a means of using capital budgeting concepts in a meaningful and feasible manner. Several problems come to mind: first that of locating a discount rate for present value calculation, second the choice of horizon for cash flow forecasts, third the means of quantifying terminal values at the horizon point, and fourth the introduction of risk measures into the calculations. Risk is distinguished from uncertainty in the accepted manner of defining a risky event as one which can be quantified in terms of known probability distributions and value measures, whereas an uncertain event lacks the means of quantitication because the probabilistic circumstances of its occurrence cannot be specified.

Possibly the credibility gap of capital budgeting models has become accentuated by the fact that models tend to be developed under restricted and simplified circumstances, typically those of full information and certainty about the future, which are acknowledged to be unrealistic. The idea that these models are *extended* to circumstances of risk and imperfect knowledge implicitly denies that it is with such circumstances that the prescriptive content of capital budgeting theory should be concerned. Until the theory or implementation of the theory improves all decision-makers face the same problems. Analogously one may say that it is only when one farmer buys a tractor that his fellow-competitor farmers who use horses need to worry – until then they all use the same method which is generally preferable to no horse at all. Thus the approach taken in this book is to acknowledge that there are problems in the application of theoretical valuation methods and management science techniques to practical analysis for acquisition decisions and therefore not to reject such methods out of hand but rather discuss their difficulties and suggest possible approaches which seem most fruitful for problem solving.

Portfolio theory and risk concepts. One area in which risk concepts have been widely analysed and incorporated into both theoretical developments and prescriptive practical applications is that of portfolio theory. The initial focus of portfolio theory was to analyse and explain the efficiency of actual equity portfolios in terms of risk-and-return combinations, on the argument that in near-perfect capital markets there would be a limiting frontier[2] of risk-and-return trade-off opportunities. In other words the market trading mechanisms and the assumption of risk aversion by investors would ensure a proportionate increase in return for increasing burdens of risk undertaken by them. Therefore investors would be found holding high risk/high return and low risk/low return portfolios but not low risk/high return portfolios nor, unless the investor was unnecessarily stupid or careless, high risk/low return portfolios.

Portfolio theory has been developed primarily for asset exchange in near-perfect markets. As such it has direct implications for acquisition financing and upon the standing of the acquirer company's equity in the stock market both before and after a deal. If overall riskiness of the acquirer's earnings is reduced one may expect that, in the absence of other changes, the rating of its equity will improve and vice versa. However, the earnings stream is a net result of product market vulnerability and investment decision results so that one will generally need to form opinions on the vulnerability of a company's product market volume and margins. Whereas security markets may be near perfect and fulfil to a great extent the underlying assumptions of portfolio theory, the product and factor markets of a company are in many cases imperfect in areas such as differential information availability to participants, differential purchasing/selling power, differential tax circumstances etc. Thus although risk-and-return ideas may be applied to product and factor markets, portfolio theory can only be justifiably applied in the domains where its assumptions are well met, namely security markets.

Risk-and-return characteristics of assets are neither generally fixed nor stationary over a period of time but tend to be influenced by many economic, political and social factors. For example property rental income has in the past provided a steady (risk-free) income stream unaffected to any major extent by business cycle factors whereas capital goods industries such as shipbuilding or machine tool manufacturing have notoriously cyclical earnings streams. On the other hand the advantages of property investment and dealing are increasingly attracting political intervention, often actuated by social unrest, which can at sudden and relatively unpredictable moments strike at the steady nature of property earnings. Therefore a narrow and short-term view of risk can be positively dangerous, but in trying to take a longer-term view inevitably one runs into the crystal ball gazing field of uncertainties. Although in no way a comprehensive means of assessing such circumstances, simulation methods can help in at least promoting awareness of the effects upon a firm of different external conditions and internal strategies. In addition capital budgeting concepts may be turned round to ask the question 'what payback period is in prospect for this project at a particular rate of interest?' rather than 'what is the net present value (or rate of return) for this project given consideration of projected cash flow over a period of (say) 10-15 years?' The general point is that at least one should make an attempt to recognize risks and uncertainties rather than shy away from them back into a make-believe world of a future known with certainty.

In noting the portfolio theory concept of risk/return trade-off, the opportunity of acquisition gain by an overall reduction in risk and/or increase in return from the acquired firm's assets in conjunction with those of the acquirer has been implied. This is reflected in a capitalization gain for the acquirer company's equity, some of which may be transmitted to the acquired firm's shareholders as part of the acquisition-financing package. In addition the acquirer company shareholders can benefit in an acquisition by bringing relative bargaining power to bear upon the negotiations. Although the City Code and proposed companies legislation will probably curb some of the more popular excesses, the advantages of bargaining from a position of relative strength can be considerable. Therefore with little management operation on the asset productivity (investment and production decisions) of the combined companies, it is possible to achieve capitalization gains (and therefore share price appreciation) by selective acquisition expansion. The operative word here is selective since there is also plenty of scope for making bad deals with adverse share price consequences. In fact underlying much of this discussion is the need for exposure to an adequate supply of acquisition opportunities and the need for extensive and accurate information about these opportunities so that sensible decisions may be made.

Search processes

If, as suggested earlier, the perspective is adopted that a firm is a complex open system engaged in interchange with its external environment, which is true almost from the nature of business enterprise, then many mechanisms of information receipt into the firm can be quickly listed. Salesmen, buyers, publications from trade associations, news media and industry meetings are all obvious sources of information relevant to acquisition decisions in addition to the conscious efforts of managers and executives to gather data about possible acquisition targets. City and professional contacts of financial executives such as stockbrokers, bankers, accountants and solicitors are important sources of potential acquisition candidates. These potential information sources could be further extended but to manage even these specific sources with a view to aiding acquisition decisions is a managerial task that demands considerable organization. Not only does a firm which wishes to pursue an acquisition strategy need to organize itself to obtain predetermined information relevant to its purposes but it also needs to recognize that for acquisition opportunities it is often the unexpected information that is important. This latter information will by definition occur at uncertain intervals and often from unplanned sources so that rigidity in information receipt organization may well be disadvantageous.

Companies which appear suitable targets for acquisition at a particular time are themselves changing with the passage of time. In addition changes in the acquirer company and the fact that many firms are engaged in pursuing expansion by acquisition mean that the search and subsequent evaluation of target companies is a dynamic process. Companies which appear attractive at one point of time may not be attractive at another and vice versa. An example of this was the proposed combination of Unilever and Allied Breweries, which after a Monopolies Commission reference and its consequential delays, proved infeasible due to relative displacements in share prices during the period of report preparation. Consequently regular monitoring of the attractions of acquiring particular target companies is necessary to aid acquisition timing.

Organization of subsequent analysis

The general discussion of this chapter has exposed the main topics which are the subject of deeper discussion in subsequent chapters. Although these topics will be treated separately, they should be seen as components of the more integrated context of the preceding discussion, to which reference will again be made in the concluding chapters.

The interrelated aspects of financing, investment and production decisions carry over into the perspectives of Chapter 2 in which acquisition strategy is considered within financial market approaches to valuation of risk and return. Following this a formalized model of financial market constraints upon acquisition financing is developed in Chapter 3. This model may be viewed as a 'satisficing' approach to the financing decision where overall optimization of financing, investment and production decisions is not a meaningful approach.

Chapter 4 provides a discussion of acquisition-bargaining concepts. It indicates opportunities for gain from bargaining both for the acquirer and the target company.

Chapter 5 elaborates upon the search process and how search and evaluation processes might be organized for an active acquisition strategy. The models in Chapters 3 and 4 are integrated into an overall model of acquisition strategy.

Finally Chapter 6 summarizes the main substance of the preceding chapters with an emphasis on prescriptive suggestions for setting and administering an acquisition strategy.

Notes

1 See for example Clarkson (1962), Cyert and March (1963), Simon (1955) and (1964) and Williamson (1967), all of which discuss problem solving and 'satisficing' behaviour by managers. Marris (1966) and Penrose (1966) are sympathetic to these concepts in development of their theories of acquisition and merger activity within corporate growth.

2 The development of portfolio theory now has an extensive literature originating with Markowitz (1959), Sharpe (1964) and Lintner (1965), and with more recent definitive articles by Jensen (1969) and Blume (1970) amongst others.

2

Financial Market Considerations

Capital market issues for acquisition analysis

Movements in share prices by which investors profit or lose are both the short- and long-term measures of the success of an acquisition decision. Given that the criterion of maximizing net present wealth of shareholders is the objective of acquisition strategy it is evidently crucial to have a suitable framework for analysing whether a proposed acquisition will be attractive to investors. The so-called 'cost of capital' to a company, which on a market view is a direct consequence of the company's capitalization, is generally regarded as the reference point for evaluating the marginal benefit of a proposed acquisition.

Cost of capital, share price movements and portfolio concepts. A short-term view of the capitalization of a publicly quoted company depends to a considerable degree upon general movements of share prices, which are assumed for the present to be outside the control of the firm. Estimation of the overall cost of capital for a company in a short-term context usually proceeds from a measure of the company's expected earnings stream in relation to its total capitalization and therefore produces a weighted average figure for the cost of debt and equity financing which fluctuates directly in relation to expected earnings and inversely in relation to debt and share price levels. If share prices move in line with expected earnings then the cost of capital measure remains fairly stable over a period of time. If it is assumed that a company's capitalization perfectly reflects revisions in expected earnings then the implicit cost of capital becomes time invariant. Some approaches to the derivation of a cost of capital effectively adopt this assumption by looking at long-run movements in company earnings yields designed to produce an average cost of capital for companies. This average cost of capital is then typically tailored to a particular company by adjustment for riskiness relative to the market average; implicit in such an adjustment lies the trade-off between risk and return in financial markets.

Discussion as to whether capitalization of companies in financial markets correctly reflects expected earnings is somewhat irrelevant since expected earnings tend to be subjective and unobservable. Attempts to relate earnings of a company year to year over a period of time have not produced relationships which offer good predictive models of earnings. Consequently direct calculation of a cost of capital to a specific company in absolute terms is not a simple exercise; in fact the subsequent discussion will argue that it is neither necessary nor relevant to calculate an absolute cost of capital figure for a company in isolation from other investment opportunities which are open to portfolio investors. Instead projected investment returns may be divided into two components, one related to overall security market returns (possibly split into components for fixed-interest stocks and equities) and the other related to the particular company's risk circumstances compared with the market. The former market component is largely independent of company decisions and results whereas the latter company component may be altered by company capital investment policy and reported results. Share price movements and therefore the concept of (marginal) cost of capital is linked to expectations; one part of the expectations relating to overall financial market price movements is not determined by any individual company management whereas the other part, which concerns expectations of existing and potential investors in a specific firm relative to the market average, may be within the control of that firm's management.

Cost of capital as an economic variable is conceptually attractive since it extends rate of interest measures into measures of return on equity shares. Portfolio theory and capital asset pricing models have developed ideas of rates of return under conditions of certainty to apply to circumstances of carefully defined risk. Overall average returns and risk in markets for particular types of securities can be calculated by evaluating risk and return on representative portfolios for those markets. The components of a specific company's risk/return profile not attributable to the overall market therefore indicates the return for a given unit of risk which investors require in relation to the market average. A further comparative measure of a company's return per unit of risk may be made against the so-called 'risk-free' interest rate which is generally associated with government bonds. Both the above measures of return per unit of risk are relative and not absolute measures. Consequently company financial strategy does not need to focus upon absolute risk/return characteristics but upon risk and return relative to other opportunities such as risk-free investment or overall investment in a representative market portfolio. More specific opportunities at industry level may be assessed by reference to representative industry portfolios.

Defining rate of return opportunities in portfolio terms in no way removes the problem that for future investment decisions expectations and not certain outcomes are being dealt with. If a portfolio viewpoint is adopted and an attempt made to measure returns per unit of risk from historical data it still requires an act of faith to assume that such a price of risk will hold for the future. The degree to which the price of risk has remained more or less steady over various historical periods for a particular portfolio will presumably influence the confidence held in such an assumption.

Predictability of share prices and risk-return considerations. Although individual company managements may be unable to control overall fluctuations in rates of interest and returns on security markets, if they were able to predict these fluctuations there would be opportunities to increase the return from capital investment decisions beyond that which could be achieved without such predictive ability. With specific reference to acquisition decisions it may be asked whether there are predictable points in time when acquisitions can be made especially favourably and if so why and in what circumstances. Suggestions have been made that acquisition activity amongst quoted companies is related to stock market cycles but no proven explanations exist for this. Certainly the bulk of evidence concerning the predictability of stock market prices weighs heavily against any successful prediction either from past price data or from econometric techniques using 'fundamental' economic series such as money supply, gross national product and similar macro-economic data. The question of random walks in stock prices has been extensively researched and it is only in the lower frequencies of several months or years and possibly the very short interdaily cycles that evidence of any non-randomness arises[1].

Emphasis has been given to risk-return relationships in essentially random markets for company fixed interest stocks and securities since acquisition analysis is essentially a dual valuation problem where the focus of analysis is upon the differences between acquirer and target companies apart and together. The risk profiles of returns to shareholders in both companies will generally alter as a result of an acquisition; from these changes derive market movements in the debt and equity instruments of the combined entity. Failure to recognize returns in association with risk either in company earnings streams or in share prices ignores some of the potential pitfalls as well as some of the opportunities for major gains which acquisition strategies can produce. Consequently this chapter first discusses the evidence concerning share price movements as a helpful background for appreciating the relevance of probabilistic returns both upon corporate valuation and valuation of more general classes of assets. Acquisitions are frequently made with a view to redeployment of a company's underlying assets rather than purely to merge and improve existing earnings streams. Comment concerning valuation of assets other than quoted securities is therefore pertinent to acquisition analysis. Cost of capital and associated investment cut-off levels are discussed in a relative sense rather than as absolute measures for each combining company in an acquisition; they cannot be divorced from risk considerations in a portfolio context.

Review of evidence concerning share price movements

The last decade has seen a sustained interest in the statistical nature of price movements in so-called 'speculative' markets. Similar studies with broadly similar results have been made covering markets for fixed interest stocks, equity shares and commodites.

Random walk model outlined

The starting point for these investigations has been the random walk model which in its common form states that the price of a share, when measured over a series of equally-spaced time intervals, and adjusted for dividends, splits and new issues, is related at one point in time to the price at the previous point in time plus an error term. Formally this is written

$$P_t = P_{t-1} + \epsilon_t \tag{1}$$

where P denotes price, ϵ denotes the error term and the suffices t denote time intervals. Interest centres on the degree to which ϵ_t and prior values of ϵ such as ϵ_{t-s} (s> 0) are related.

For example if

$$\epsilon_t = a\epsilon_{t-1}$$

then

$$P_t - P_{t-1} = a(P_{t-1} - P_{t-2})$$

so that

$$P_t = (1 + a)P_{t-1} - aP_{t-2}$$

which if a is non-zero allows one to predict future prices from past prices. On the other hand if a is zero then the best predictor of the next price is simply the current price. If it can be shown that the statistical distribution of ϵ_t is such that it has a zero average value and no covariance between ϵ_t and ϵ_{t-s} (s> 0) then this constitutes evidence favourable to the random walk notion that future share prices cannot be predicted solely from past share prices; Figure 2:1 illustrates the point.

The parameter a is the average relationship between past price changes and the disturbance term is the 'random' influence between observed changes. A random walk therefore will have an average value. In the context of share price predictability for the purposes of profitable trading, the average or trend will only be useful if it is non-zero. Essentially the random walk hypothesis of share price movements is that prices follow a random walk without trend for a wide range of observation intervals between the short term (eg daily intervals) to the longer term (eg monthly movements).

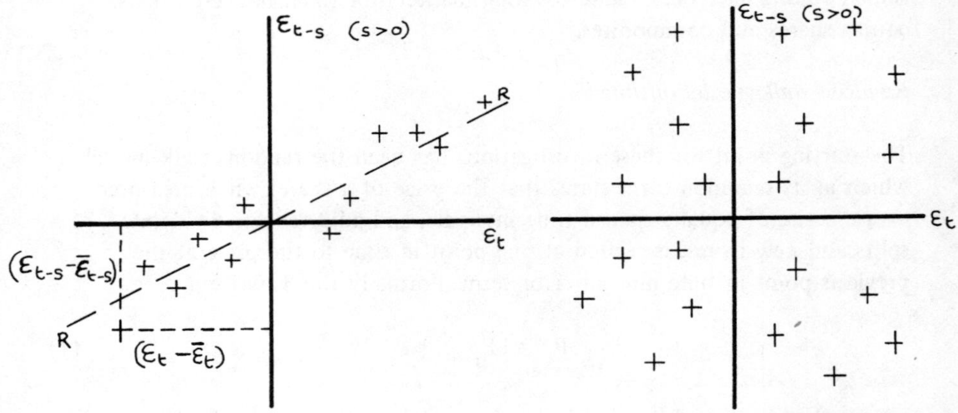

High covariance between $\varepsilon_{t\text{-}s}$ and ε_t. A regression line RR fits the data well.

Low covariance between $\varepsilon_{t\text{-}s}$ and ε_t. No meaningful regression line can be fitted.

Figure 2:1 Covariance between random walk disturbance terms

Considerations of symmetry in statistical distributions make it preferable to analyse the logarithms of price movements as opposed to the absolute price changes since the logarithm of a price change to zero is negative infinity, the logarithm of an infinitely large price change is plus infinity, and the logarithm of an unchanged price is zero. Thus the random walk model which is normally tested takes the form

$$\log P_t = \log P_{t-1} + \eta_t \tag{2}$$

where η_t is a residual error term with similar characteristics as ϵ_t. The models (1) and (2) are practically the same for small price changes but the emphasis of the logarithmic firm is upon proportionate rather than absolute price changes; indeed the former is of greater relevance to investment-decision criteria which focus upon return to some level of invested funds.

Plots of the distribution of $(\log P_t - \log P_{t-1})$, ie the distribution of η_t, for time series of share prices or prices in many other speculative markets, tend to produce very similarly shaped graphs. These histograms of price changes may be well approximated by particular statistical distributions which can be fitted to the histogram data. An example from the author's research in commodity markets is shown in Figure 2:2; similar results for share price fluctuations have been widely reported, for example by Fama (1970) and Mandelbrot (1963), (1967). The actual 'best fit' theoretical distribution, of which two possibilities are shown in Figure 2:2, is still the subject of much academic discussion. The illustration shows both a normal distribution, the flatter curve, and a 'stable Paretian' distribution which has a somewhat more peaked centre and fatter tails than the normal; mathematically the normal is a special case of the stable Paretian. The stable Paretian distribution was fitted to the data using procedures outlined by Fama and Roll (1968), (1971) following the work of Mandelbrot who showed that stable Paretian distributions offered good models of speculative market price movements. The author's results for commodity markets and results by other researchers for shares and other speculative markets indicate that for practical purposes the distributions of logged price changes are symmetrical once the sample trend has been removed.

Investment horizon and definition of trend. In any sample distribution of a series of share price changes similar to that of Figure 2:2 it is likely that the mean will have some non-zero value. Over particular time periods it will be possible to say statistically that the mean has a value significantly or not-significantly different from zero. In the former case the price series may be said to have a trend and in the latter no trend. The basic random walk model of share price movements postulates the lack of a trend and indeed the majority of the evidence supports this, at least in series of daily and monthly price movements. However the question of existence of trends is largely a value judgment from the analyst's viewpoint in that it depends upon his horizon and sample periods. A sample taken from a bull market will quite possibly indicate a significant rising trend in weekly observed price date; the same data over a bull and bear market together will probably indicate no significant trend. Very long-term observations at quarterly or annual intervals tend to show a long-term slightly rising trend in stock market prices.

The investment horizon naturally varies with investor purposes. Short-term speculators may be interested in price movements over periods of months whereas the longer-term fund manager of a pension fund or life office may take a much more distant horizon of several years. Figure 2:3 indicates mean and standard deviation figures for different length observation samples made on daily data for silver prices during 1968 – 1973.

The results show that the mean and standard deviation measures (ex-post) varied substantially from sample period to sample period and in no very obvious manner. Ex-ante it would have been very desirable for trading purposes to know what price movement distribution covered the next period; in other words would it have been possible to predict the distribution from which the next sample was subsequently found to have been derived, even if it is accepted that price changes over the sample period move only randomly in conformity with the particular distribution? Unfortunately this poses the

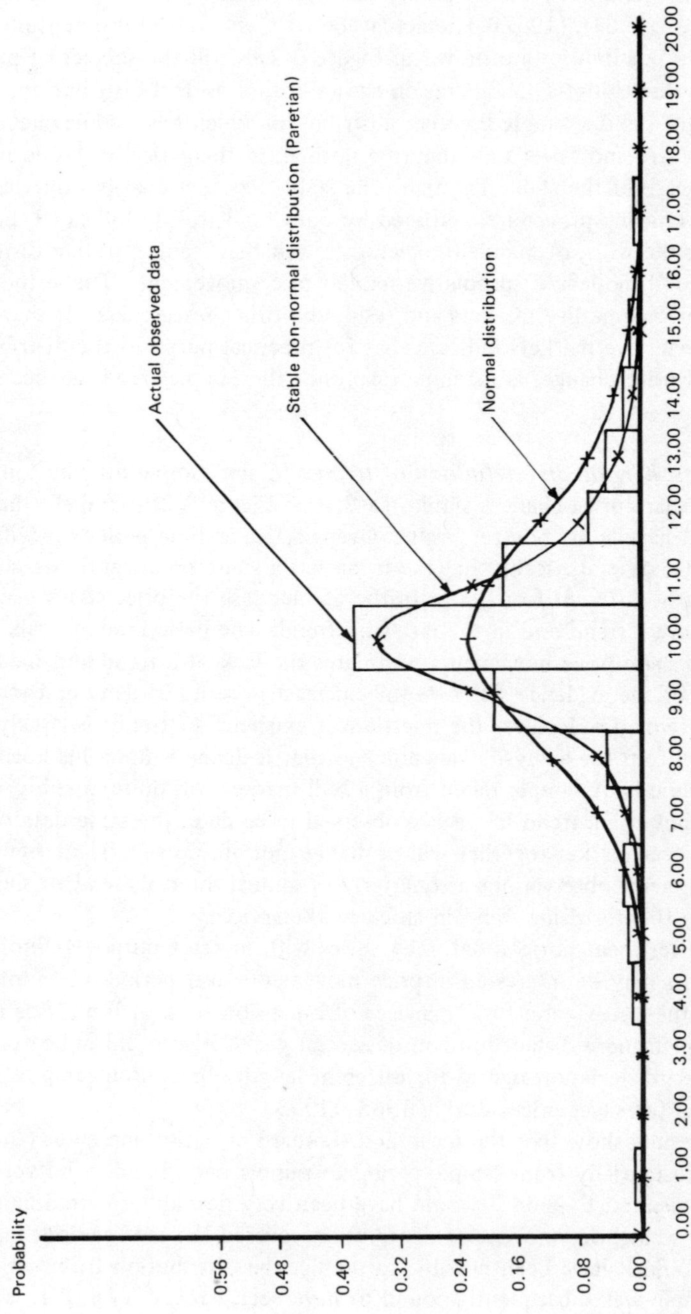

Figure 2:2 Distributions of price movements in speculative markets

question as to whether the distribution function which best fits observed price changes is stationary or not, ie whether the parameters of the function change significantly in course of time and if so whether they change in any predictable manner. These questions have not yet been researched in any depth, but the general aim of seeking cyclical patterns in price movements has been extensively researched by spectral analysis methods without detecting any clear patterns in the longer term other than a slight upward drift of share prices – see Granger and Morgenstern (1970).

Distribution of η *in share price random walk.* The question of what distribution of period-to-period price changes, at least for daily and weekly price data, best fits the random walk model is still controversial. Distributions of price changes have longer tails and more peaked centres than can be explained by straightforward normal distributions. The stable Paretian model has exceptionally long tails which inevitably contain more probability weight than any finite sample of realized data to which they may be fitted. Two issues in particular arise concerning best fit distributions. First, is there a theoretical distribution which should fit price movement data and second, what known distribution actually offers the best explanation? At present there is no widely accepted theory of price change generation in speculative markets, although Granger and Morgenstern discuss a number of interesting propositions particularly in connection with the relationship of trading volume and high, low prices and concerning the influence upon interdaily price movements of floor traders in US stock exchanges. The second issue, as to what distribution actually offers the best fit to data, depends to some extent upon the objectives of the analyst. If the analyst is prepared to consider that there are 'exceptional' price changes which should be removed from the price data series prior to fitting a distribution then the long-tailed distributions may be inappropriate. On the other hand if the observer regards unusual (infrequent perhaps) price changes as simply an integral part of the price movement process then the long-tailed distributions would appear attractive. Mandelbrot (1969) found that many other economic, agricultural and meteorological time series phenomena exhibit long-tailed distributions to which the stable Paretian models offers a good fit. The main point to make is that if risk is defined in terms of variability about some average figure then the choice of distribution can have a considerable influence upon measures of potential gains and losses.

Financial market risk and the random walk model. To illustrate this, consider the projection of daily price movements over a three-month period based upon distribution parameters of various progressively longer-tailed distributions in the stable Paretian class of which the normal is one instance[2]. Figure 2:5 illustrates the confidence limits for three different distributions parameters at various time horizons of up to three months within which prices will probably fluctuate from a starting point of 100. All distributions have a zero trend and the same scale parameter c but differ in their ('characteristic exponent') parameter, α. In research on stock market prices it has been found that fitting stable Paretian distributions to price series generally yields α values in the range $1.6 \leqslant \alpha \leqslant 2.0$, where the case of $\alpha = 2.0$ produces a normal distribution. The results for $\alpha = 1.6$ are plotted out for illustrative purposes in Figure 2:4.

	250 Observations		400 Observations		1 000 Observations	
	Mean	Standard Deviation	Mean	Standard Deviation	Mean	Standard Deviation
Sample 1	-.032	2.05	-.017	1.79	-.043	1.44
2	+.013	1.19	-.027	1.17		
3	-.086	1.24	+.018	1.12		
4	-.026	1.08				
5	+.134	1.08				
Implicit Horizon	1 year		1.6 years		4 years	

Figure 2:3 Statistics for daily price movements in the silver market

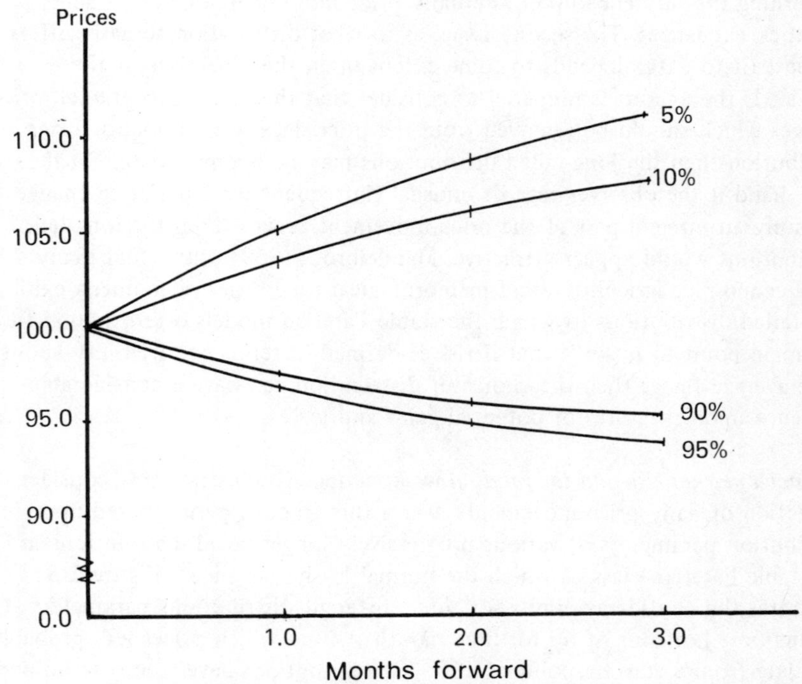

Figure 2:4 Confidence limits on price levels for α = 1.6

The values in Figure 2:5 were simulated using the Fama and Roll generating process noted earlier. Numerical values are illustrative of the effect of various feasible a values. If the scale coefficient was larger/smaller the 'fanning-out' of the various confidence limit price levels would be greater/smaller in proportion to the exponential of the scale parameter. The lack of symmetry of the fan about the 100.0 price level is due to the effect of a logged-price random walk model. It is worth noting that an a level of 1.6 as against a normal distribution ($a = 2.0$) more than doubles the fanning-out of the confidence limits and an a level of 1.8 increases the fanning-out by 50%. These proportions directly reflect increased variability and therefore risk in the random walk process.

	Confidence limits	Forward price levels at confidence limits: 1 month	2 months	3 months	Scale parameter at 3 months
	5%	105.3	108.3	110.8	
	10%	103.8	105.9	107.7	
$a = 1.6$					0.032
	90%	97.5	96.1	95.0	
	95%	96.6	94.8	93.3	
	5%	103.2	104.9	106.2	
	10%	102.5	103.8	104.8	
$a = 1.8$					0.022
	90%	98.2	97.3	96.7	
	95%	97.6	96.5	95.6	
	5%	102.3	103.3	104.0	
	10%	101.9	102.7	103.3	
$a = 2.0$					0.016
(normal	90%	98.7	98.1	97.6	
distribution)	95%	98.3	97.5	97.0	

Notes: Figures given relate to projections of a distribution of a random walk observed at four times a day with a scale parameter of 0.002 for the quarter-day distribution.
There is no trend in the distributions.
Base price level at time zero is 100.0. This corresponds to the 50% confidence level throughout the horizon.
The distributions are projected up to three months ahead.
The scale parameter is given for the distribution at three months forward from the base point.
Price levels are in absolute prices whereas the underlying distributions relate to logged prices.

Figure 2:5 Confidence limit price levels for different a values for stable Paretian distributions

Random walk implications for investment analysis. Lest confusion arises about the implications and claims of the random walk model, which is important to subsequent parts of the discussion, it is worth noting Granger and Morgenstern's summary of what the random walk model does *not* say[3].

1 The random walk model is concerned with the absolute price of stock X in the future given only a history of the prices of stock X in the past. It is not concerned with relative price changes with respect to indices, other shares etc.
2 The work of the investment analyst is not pointless in so far as he seeks to produce forecasts of relative price changes rather than absolute price levels. Most analysts are concerned with analysing relative merits of respective stocks, for example such problems as selection of the best stock in the construction sector.
3 The random walk model is only concerned with prices and does not assume or imply that the stock market necessarily approximates to one of perfect competition.
4 It is not a theoretically derived model but offers a good approximation to a large number of price series over a wide range of time intervals.
5 The random walk does not infer that past information is of no use in assessing distributions of future price changes. With stationary distribution parameters, past returns would provide the best means of assessing distributions of future returns.

The random walk results do tend to discredit the short-term absolute price forecasting claims of share price chartists. Only perhaps in the longer-term periods over several months or years may the chartist concepts of patterns which indicate trend changes or breakthrough of trend lines be significant. Conceivably it may be possible to establish some link between such trend change indicators with non-stationarity of random walk distributions. In this, the problem of selection of investment horizons reappears in that apparent non-stationarity may just be a realization of a further underlying random or non-random process. The point is largely academic since testing such a proposition would require extremely long data series. However, the random walk model does not preclude chartists from constructing implicit price forecasting models from several charts, eg charts of interest rates, share price indices and exchange rates, and thereby being able to make useful predictions; unfortunately the models have not been formalized and tested in any rigorous manner analogous to econometric models for example. It would be most interesting to analyse whether distribution parameters of price changes bear any relationship to chartist trend and trend reversal measures over any periods chosen by chartists and if so whether as a result successful predictions could be generated; given present evidence the likelihood of producing useful predictive models based upon charts seems remote.

It might reasonably be thought that absolute price levels of shares would relate to earnings and dividend forecasts. A number of studies, mainly using US data, have shown as one might expect that share price levels are positively related to dividends and earnings, ie higher dividends and earnings are associated with higher share prices. The studies relate to prices, dividends and earnings across several shares for a particular point in time. This may be gratifying in a historical sense but it does not help to forecast price levels as it would be necessary to first predict either dividends or earnings. There is some scope for dividend predictability over a period of time probably because company boards are reluctant to reduce dividends year to year, but research into the relationship of future company earnings with past earnings has not indicated any scope for predictive purposes[4]. It may be conjectured that whereas dividends are a cash flow measure of returns to shareholders, reported earnings suffer from all the variations in practice of accruals accounting and in recent years have become an increasingly less consistent measure across companies due to the differential impact of inflation. On the other hand if a company adopts a consistent basis of earnings reporting over a period of time then the measure may be a reasonable statistical proxy for cash flow earnings in time series analysis specific to the company.

Share prices and reaction to new information. A further topic of interest concerns the speed with which the stock market reacts to fresh information, the process often being referred to as 'discounting' of new information in share prices. Both theoretical and practical studies have been made on this subject, which is of specific interest to acquisition analysis in connection with access to unpublished or little known information and the effect of 'leaks' prior to the public announcement of an acquisition. At a theoretical level Samuelson (1965) has shown that given an assumption of some true or intrinsic levels of a share price, such as valuations based upon discounted future dividend flows which change in relation to new information reaching the market, then the actual price series would conform approximately to a random walk. For this approximation new information about a stock would need to reach the market fairly irregularly – as for example do dividend and earnings announcements.

Empirical evidence of the speed of adjustment of prices to new information, specifically stock splits, has been discussed by Fama, Fisher, Jensen and Roll (1969) who conclude that prices on the New York Stock Exchange adjust within the month of the split to reflect new anticipations of dividends associated with the split. Evidence that stock prices reflect the price implications of annual earnings announcements and new issues within a very short time, almost certainly less than one month, from the date of public announcement, has been noted by Fama (1970); his findings also suggest that much of the related price movement occurs prior to the respective announcement dates. Evidence also consistent with rapid discounting of new information into share prices comes from Fitzgerald's study of the share price movements in response to brokers' circulars[5]. This indicates that circulars from brokers can have a direct effect on share prices within a matter of weeks. Overall it is now fairly well established that prices in stock markets do adjust quickly to new information and to this extent stock markets are generally regarded as 'efficient' markets. However definition of information is an open issue; considerably more research is required to categorize information that reaches investors into its degree of relevance in terms of effect upon share price movements.

Fundamental models for absolute price forecasting

The random walk model is largely unconcerned with how information reaches stock markets and is translated into price movements but, following the prior discussion, focuses upon the nature of price movements alone and the consistency of such price movements with rapid discounting of information. Consequently the random walk model does not preclude the possibility of forecasting price movements if fundamental causal mechanisms by which price movements are formed can be uncovered. Unfortunately there are both practical and logical reasons for doubting the feasibility of achieving useful forecasts over any meaningful time period. No doubt models have been and will be constructed which successfully forecast absolute prices over particular finite time periods but good reasons exist why successful price level forecasting is a difficult aim to achieve and probably a matter of luck. This also applies to analysis of turning points which are concerned with change in direction of trends.

Share prices, monetary data and business confidence. One difficulty is associated with the good information discounting mechanisms of the stock market. Not only do share prices quickly discount company specific information, they also discount macro-economic fluctuations with a similarly short response lag. Evidence to support this comes from a study by the author of correlations amongst UK macro-economic variables and the Financial Times 500 Share Index. Both quarterly and some monthly data over the period 1964 – 1969 were used in various ordinary least-squares regressions. The level of, and changes in, the 500 Share Index were examined with respect to macro-economic variables both singly and in multiple-regression models. Essentially the exercise was a pilot study to consider the feasibility of building an econometric model for forecasting absolute levels of share prices with a particular emphasis on monetary data. The results are summarized in Figure 2:6.

It is interesting to note that balance of payments and crude steel production (a measure of economic activity) were not significantly associated with the Index or changes in the Index. It is fully recognized that more extensive model building based upon macro-economic theory might have altered the significant variables and extended them. However none of these variables showed any evidence of a lead over the 500 Index which would be required for predictive purposes.

Variables significantly* correlated with the absolute level of the 500 Share Index

Money supply
London Clearing Bank advances outstanding
London Clearing Bank deposits outstanding
London Clearing Bank & Accepting House advances outstanding
Gross National Product
Gross domestic capital formation
Net new orders
Index of house prices
Stock Exchange turnover transactions/business day
Consols index
Building Society advances
Source of capital funds
Loans and mortgages to persons by other financial institutions

Variables significantly* correlated with changes (first differences) in the 500 Share Index

Money supply
Changes in London Clearing Bank advances outstanding
Changes in London Clearing Bank & Accepting House advances outstanding
Building Society advances
Stock Exchange turnover £/business day
Loans and mortgages to persons by other financial institutions
Bank lending to personal private sector and loans and mortgages to persons by other financial institutions

* Significant here means a 95% confidence limit in the correlations/regressions for the t-test on individual independent variables

Figure 2:6

The study also included monthly data over a shorter period for indices of business attitudes based upon the Financial Times monthly surveys of business opinion during the period April 1967 – June 1969. It was found that indices based upon business confidence and capital investment intentions were correlated with the 500 Share Index. Again there was no lead of either of these attitude series over the 500 Share Index. Furthermore the published data of business attitudes or of macro-economic data inevitably come out some time after events (most macro-economic data is compiled on a quarterly basis) whereas share price movements are instantaneously reported; thus predictive models would require more than a quarterly lead merely to provide current period predictions.

The preceding results are shown largely to suggest that evidence of the discounting effect in share prices is not confined to company specific information and that it is clearly a hard task to predict share price levels which appear (as one might expect) to be a leading variable in the economy.

'Open systems' implications for models of share price movements. Another difficulty concerns the 'open-system' nature of the forces which determine share price changes. At the 'micro'-level it would be possible to examine the actions of each investor and possibly construct some model of the main processes which make him take decisions to invest, disinvest or not to alter his Stock Exchange positions. Although economic factors such as available cash and credit, alternative investment opportunities and risk preferences would tend to be obvious explanatory components of such a model it might be found that additional sociological and psychological influences are of significance. Segregation of investors into categories such as fund managers and private investors, and segregation by investment horizons, may show up significantly different criteria for investment selection. Identification of such categories would be important to facilitate building from the 'micro' to the 'macro' by an aggregation process with a view to simulating behaviour in the large as a composition of behaviour patterns in the small[6]. Intuitively it is possible to appreciate the enormous range of influences that could be identified as having some effect on investor activities.

Macro-economic models are concerned with aggregates and assume that the impact of all effects other than those specified in the model is small. The extent to which a particular model fits the data from which it is estimated reflects the relative importance of included and excluded variables; if a model of GNP explains 90% of the variation in GNP over a period of time then the remaining 10% is by definition due to variations in excluded effects. If the structure of the economy remained the same in course of time and the importance of included variables did not change either amongst themselves or relative to excluded variables then the model would continue to achieve a 90% degree fit to future events. However in practice an economy is a dynamic system and responds to influences in ways which do not remain stationary through time. Furthermore because an economy is not a closed system, and has a structure which changes in course of time – for example, increases in union bargaining power have almost certainly altered the relationship between unemployment and wage inflation – it is improbable that a model fitted to historical data will achieve a good fit for the future. The best that can be done is to estimate a model from past data, assume that the near future will be similar, in terms of structure and importance of excluded to included variables, and then simulate the future under a range of possible circumstances. The results of such an exercise are unavoidably a value judgment of the researcher irrespective of the objectivity with which the underlying model has been built or the regularity with which it is updated to fit most recent data.

In summary, whilst the idea can be conceived of building fundamental models to explain historical share price movements, the likelihood of being able to use them for predictive purposes is not large. Two reasons for this have been discussed, first that share prices tend to be a leading variable in the economy and second that, since the stock market is an open system *par excellence* in terms of the potential influences upon investor decision making, it is unlikely that those variables which will most affect share price movements in the future can be identified.

Portfolio considerations for acquisition decisions

Given the objective of overall net present wealth maximization for shareholders in the acquirer company, acquisition strategy should aim to improve the risk-return position of shareholders. Levy and Sarnat (1970) have raised the interesting question as to whether there is any point at all in management of an individual company adopting such an aim when shareholders can adjust their portfolios amongst quoted securities to achieve desired risk-return positions without management of individual companies taking acquisitive action. In an efficient stock market without taxes or transaction costs and without management-dependent profitability this would indeed be the case. Even in markets where there are transaction costs and taxes on share transfers it might still favour shareholders to adjust their portfolios rather than have management make acquisitions. This would be the case if the acquisition transaction costs such as fees to merchant banks, solicitors, accountants etc exceeded portfolio adjustment costs and no returns accrued as a result of the combination additional to those of the combining companies.

The Levy and Sarnat argument will not apply in practice if the acquirer management achieves additional returns from the acquired company assets (eg if economies of scale are realized), if shareholders are not maximizing their risk-return position in financial markets, or if there are one or more shareholders who cannot readily adjust their portfolios except by altering the company's investments. A case in point would be a controlling family trust which cannot borrow against the security of its investment in the firm nor sell its holding. Another instance would be a management team whose members have no wealth other than their shareholdings which are financed by a merchant bank with understandings as to transfer rights. A pilot study of UK shareholder habits by Chesham Research Unit (1971) suggests that private individuals are fairly passive in their portfolio adjustment habits; however, in the absence of comparative information one cannot state this as a conclusive fact. Overall it is therefore assumed that acquisitions can frequently benefit a company's shareholders over and above benefits which they can achieve from individual portfolio adjustment in financial markets; this is especially the case where transformation and improvement of the acquired firm's earnings is possible through managerial action post-acquisition or through exercise of monopolistic power in the purchase of shares – see Chapter 4 under 'Market operations'.

A discussion of the risk-return position of individual companies in a portfolio context is relevant to acquisition strategy in that it can indicate the type of acquisition which may be expected to prove attractive to investors and therefore beneficial in terms of share price appreciation. Furthermore portfolio concepts link with capital budgeting objectives to suggest the acquisition investment decision criteria which company managements should adopt. The development of portfolio theory may be followed through a number of papers, especially Sharpe (1964), Lintner (1965) and Jensen (1969), although only the results will be discussed here.

Basic portfolio theory concepts. It is necessary to recognize that, changes in general price levels excepted, there are securities such as government bonds which have almost risk-free characteristics. Default on them is negligible and thus the variance on the return is nil. There is a gradation in terms of risk through bonds and debentures of various kinds to preference and finally ordinary shares over which risk increases. Risk here means the variance of the return about some anticipated value which is generally taken as the mean or expected value of future returns for a chosen horizon period. The nature of financial markets ensures that investors can invest their funds in combinations of investments which can contain risk-free as well as risky assets and which may be financed in part by borrowings. Profit-maximizing investors would always seek to achieve maximum return for a given risk or minimal risk for a given return consistent with their particular indifference curves, which are assumed to be risk-averse. Consequently it can be shown that there are boundaries of so-called 'efficient' portfolios, ie the best attainable portfolios for various categories of investors. For investment in risky assets alone, in the absence of the ability to lend or borrow at the risk-free interest rate R , the efficient boundary is given by APMQB in Figure 2:7. If lending and borrowing at the risk-free rate are feasible then the efficient boundary is line RSMC.

The main assumptions of portfolio theory are that distributions of returns on individual assets and portfolios are described by a two-parameter distribution (which must be the normal), that investors prefer higher to lower expected future wealth, and that they are risk-averse. Curves I^x_1, I^x_2 and I^y_1, I^y_2, therefore, are respective indifference contours for risk-averse investors X and Y. Curves I^x_2, I^y_2 reflect their best opportunities for investment in risky assets alone whereas I^x_1, I^y_1 reflect their best opportunities of investing in risky assets, together with investing or borrowing at the risk-free interest rate R. Investor X achieves point S by a combination of risk-free investment at R plus risky investment at M whilst investor Y achieves point C by a combination of borrowing at the risk-free rate R and risky investment at M.

The point M is that achieved by the so-called 'market portfolio', namely a portfolio which contains all risky assets each in proportion to its fraction of the total value of all securities. If the market was not in equilibrium then prices of securities in the market (efficient) portfolio would be bid up by buyers and prices of securities not in M would fall until all securities were held.

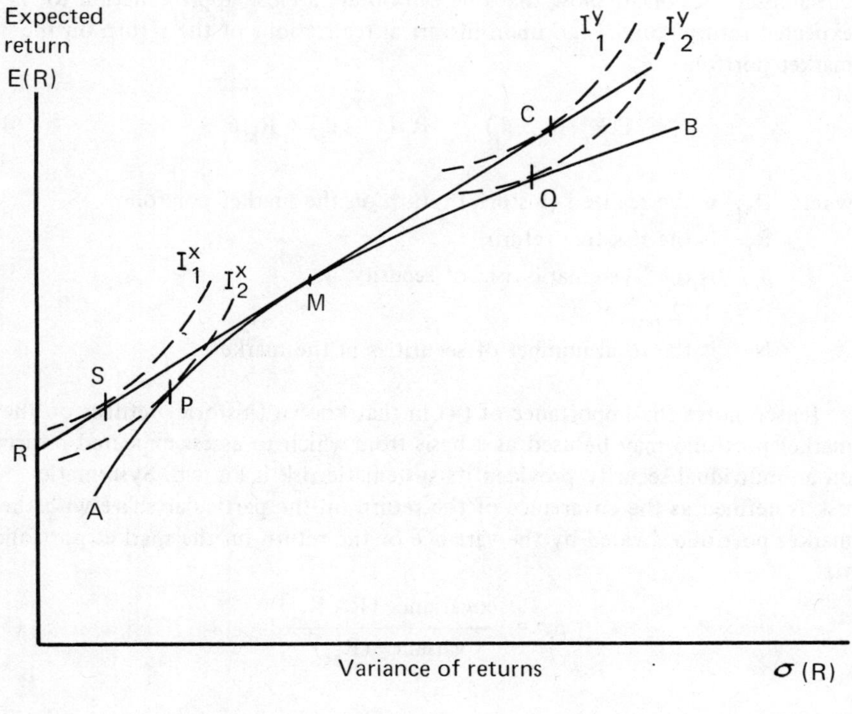

Figure 2:7 Portfolio theory concepts of risk and return

Returns on a security or portfolio. The return on a share over a particular time horizon may be defined in terms of the share price change (adjusted for capital alterations where necessary) together with dividend receipts over the period. Formally

$$R_t = \frac{P_t + D_t}{P_{t-1}}$$

where D_t is the dividend received ($\geqslant 0$) in the period t, R_t is the total return and P is the share price at the end of each period. A logarithmic form could also be used.

It is generally assumed that a linear relationship exists between the return on the jth share and the overall market portfolio, so that over a time interval

$$R_j = E(R_j) + b_j\pi + e_j \tag{3}$$

where $E(R_j)$ is the expected return on the stock, π is the 'market factor', b_j is a constant and e_j is an error term. The underlying assumptions of this model are fully explained in Jensen (1969); in particular π and e_j are assumed to be normally distributed. As stated the model involves *expectations* but Jensen goes on to show that one can obtain a close approximation to the expected return *conditional* upon historical realizations of the return on the market portfolio:

$$E(R_j \mid R_M, \beta_j) \simeq R_F(1 - \beta_j) + R_M\beta_j \tag{4}$$

where R_M is the realized (historic) return on the market portfolio
R_F is the risk-free return
β_j is the 'systematic risk' of security j
$j = 1, 2 \ldots N$
N is the total number of securities in the market.

Jensen notes the importance of (4) in that known (historic) returns on the market portfolio may be used as a basis from which to assess expected returns on an individual security provided its systematic risk is known. Systematic risk is defined as the covariance of the return on the particular share with the market portfolio divided by the variance of the return on the market portfolio, viz:

$$\beta_j = \frac{\text{covariance}\ (R_j, R_M)}{\text{variance}\ (R_M)} \tag{5}$$

The systematic risk enables one to measure the risk of the jth security relative to the market portfolio and extends to measures of systematic risk for combinations, ie portfolios, of securities relative to the market portfolio.

The random walk model of price movements in speculative markets has implications for the market model variables π and e. The earlier discussion concerning the distribution of share price changes period to period showed that the observed distributions tended not to be normal but to have longer tails better fitted by the stable Paretian model. Consequently it is of interest to establish whether the non-normality of observed price changes has severe effects for the results (4) and (5) which assume normally distributed returns/price movements in security markets. Jensen has investigated the effect of stable Paretian distributions upon portfolio theory and has shown that analogous formulae apply to the stable Paretian case although β relates to statistical measures different from covariance and variance. In fact the stable Paretian model has no covariance or variance except in the special case when its characteristic exponent is 2.0, ie it becomes a normal distribution. Jensen also argued that measures of systematic risk, which are derived for investors with identical horizons, can be extended to markets where investors have different horizons and trading in securities takes place on a continuous basis (see Jensen (1969), pp. 186-92).

The effect of departures from normality in price distributions can be illustrated by considering the degree of dispersion of portfolio returns as the number of shares in a portfolio is increased. Risk-averse behaviour would seek the lowest dispersion of returns consistent with other costs of diversification. Following Fama (1965), the values of dispersion (related to the scale parameter c of Figure 2:5) are tabulated for different values of the characteristic exponent (a) and the number of shares in a portfolio (n). From the results in Figure 2:8 it is clear that diversification has greater effect, ie returns become increasingly certain, both as n increases and as a increases. In fact, diversification provides an effective means of decreasing the variability of returns on a portfolio over the range of a values that are likely to be encountered in practice. Having shown that portfolio theoretic concepts are appropriate to the longer-tailed stable Paretian models of price movements, albeit less effective than if price movement distributions are normally distributed, the somewhat simpler variance/covariance portfolio model will be used in subsequent discussion of its implications for acquisition strategies.

a	n			
	1	10	100	1 000
1.60	2	1.251	1.063	1.016
1.80	2	1.158	1.025	1.004
2.00 (normal)	2	1.10	1.010	1.001

Figure 2:8 Values of dispersion of portfolio returns for different a and n

Present portfolio selection theory implies a once-for-all selection procedure. In practice investors adjust portfolios by degrees, especially the larger investment funds which could experience difficulty in buying or selling complete shareholdings at (marginal) quoted prices. Practical portfolio adjustment is therefore a dynamic marginal decision process which considers only a subset of investment opportunities at one time rather than the full range on a continuing basis. This does not preclude a marginal adjustment process with an incomplete analysis of the range of investment opportunities from creating portfolios close to the efficient frontier (line RSMC of Figure 2:7) since efficient portfolios may be constructed from various combinations of investments. Indeed Jensen's tests of portfolios assembled by US mutual funds showed that the portfolios were well diversified.

Although a company's current earnings are a poor proxy for its future earnings capability, for comparative purposes it would seem reasonable to compare price-earnings ratios of selected equity groups as an indicator of expectations concerning relative growth and volatility of earnings. Figure 2:9 shows that property and investment trust groups have had consistently higher ratings than industrial shares. This is by no means unexpected from a portfolio viewpoint in that earnings from property rentals and from investment trust diversified portfolios, possibly with overseas contents, offer earnings streams which are less correlated with general domestic economic events than individual industrial shares and are therefore more highly valued.

The price-earnings ratio reflects the market capitalization of an earnings stream which has both volatility and growth components. Figure 2:9 covers both a bullish and a bearish phase of a stock market cycle and should be considered only as an indication of relative sector average capitalizations. Given a viewpoint concerned with relative price-earnings multiples, there is no conflict with random walk implications.

Summary. The foregoing discussion suggests that an acquisition strategy should start with the question What constitutes a valuable change to portfolio investors which can be brought about within existing management and physical resource constraints? Given that equilibrating influences operate quickly in the stock market then the effects of a change will be quickly realized in share price adjustment and consequently in capitalization of the firm. The only beneficial changes to shareholders will be:

1 Increased expectations of return for the same risk
2 Reduced risk for the same expected return
3 Some advantageous trade-off between risk and return.

And, as argued at the start of this section, in general mere combination of companies without scope for managerially originated changes can be carried out by portfolio action of shareholders without the need for acquisitions. In terms of Figure 2:7 it is necessary for investors to expect that the combined companies will achieve a better location on the risk-return plane than any existing portfolio of shares in the two combining companies can achieve.

Sector P/E ratios	as at 31 December			
	1970	1971	1972	1973
Industrial groups	14.21	19.51	18.03	11.02
Investment trusts	29.74	36.51	38.67	25.31
Property groups	32.77	43.68	39.05	26.87

Figure 2:9 Price-earnings ratios of certain equity groups

Perspectives on valuation of assets and companies for acquisition

Portfolio theory has demonstrated how security assets can be combined to form optimal portfolios. Portfolio adjustment results in security pricing which reflects expectations of returns and the variability of those returns. Thus given a risk-free rate of return the price of other assets and securities may be determined provided the market for them is consistent with portfolio theory assumptions. Determination of the risk-free interest rate lies outside the scope of this discussion and should be seen as a process of macro-economic adjustment at a national and increasingly an international level. Evidence of price movements in security markets suggests that they are to a large degree efficient in terms of response to information and that portfolio theoretic concepts may be meaningfully employed. Since relevant information to investors is made available in widely publicized form and there are many buyers and sellers who in general do not have opportunities of controlling prices one may regard security markets as conforming well to the economic concept of a perfectly competitive market.

Capitalization and cash flow expectations

It is perhaps unfortunate that capital budgeting methods have been extended from valuation of internal capital investments to valuation of quoted companies without due consideration of the differences between absolute and marginal valuation. Attempts to reach an 'intrinsic' value of a company rather than a valuation relative to other companies have introduced something of a red herring into the problems of corporate valuation. Any investment project is a marginal decision which should be compared with some alternative opportunity within a market context for the returns available to ownership of the firm. Security markets are concerned with expectations and thus it is the change in investor expectations that is crucial in assessing the advantages or disadvantages of an acquisition. Although formulation of the capital budgeting model concerns absolute measures it can be used in a comparative manner and as a way of interpreting profits made by shareholders due to revision of expectations.

It is pertinent to follow the description of cash flow 'profit' outlined by Bodenhorn (1964) as a mean of demonstrating the link between changes in share price, and therefore shareholder wealth, due to changes in expectations. Specifically

$$S_0 = \frac{N_1}{(1+r)} + \frac{N_2}{(1+r)^2} + \text{ to infinity } = \sum_{i=1}^{\infty} \frac{N_i}{(1+r)^i} \qquad (6)$$

where S_0 is the shareholders' initial investment
N_i is the expected net cash flow in the ith future period
r is the discount rate appropriate to the share and is determined in financial markets.

The expected end-of-period wealth of shareholders $E(W_1)$ is provided by a similar expression to (6) but moved forward one period in time:

$$E(W_1) = N_1 + \frac{N_2}{(1+r)} + \frac{N_3}{(1+r)^2} \text{ to infinity } = S_0(1+r)$$

The actual end-of-period wealth W_1 will be defined in terms of the share value at the end of the first period based upon a revised set of expected cash flows M_i, from the second period onwards together with the cash flow to shareholders C_1 during the first period.

$$W_1 = C_1 + \frac{M_2}{(1+r)} + \frac{M_3}{(1+r)^2} \ldots = C_1 + \sum_{i=2}^{\infty} \frac{M_i}{(1+r)^{i-1}}$$

If expectations N_i had been correct then $C_1 = N_1$ and $M_i = N_i$. In the event of changed expectations then a 'pure' cash flow would result in

$$W_1 - E(W_1) = W_1 - S_0(1+r)$$

The discount rate here reflects the financial market judgment of the time value of money plus some risk element of return which is analogous to the economic idea of a normal return. Bodenhorn continues with an analysis of the effects of differences between accruals and cash flow profit measures; extensive examples of such effects and a comprehensive treatment of company-discounted cash flow models can be found in capital budgeting and company valuation texts[7]. Evidently. beneficial acquisitions should both raise expectations of investors and subsequently realize cash flows in accordance with those expectations.

Returns from underlying assets

Whilst evidence and theory of competitive financial markets for stocks and shares indicates objectives for acquisition strategy in terms of risk and return, ultimately expectation formation at company level concerns the deployment of underlying assets such as land and capital assets, labour and materials. Included in such resource categories are land, factories, offices, plant, machinery, transportation equipment, inventories, labour, managers etc. The acquisition analyst is faced with the need to assess the effect upon returns to investors contingent upon revised expectations of cash flows from assets in the combining companies. Decisions concerning asset deployment will frequently involve comparison of 'going-concern' and 'break-up' valuations; the former being a valuation of future achievable cash flow incomes and the latter being an assessment of current realizable values. Both going-concern and break-up asset values can be handled by the capital budgeting framework since the present value of an asset under conditions of equilibrium in asset markets would be the discounted future earnings stream derivable from the asset.

Formality of exchange aspects. Progressively greater difficulty exists in valuation of non-security assets as the formality of exchange decreases. For example formalized commodity exchanges specify delivery date, quality, quantity and tender methods which are recognized by buyer and seller. Markets in domestic, industrial and commercial property are relatively well defined; recognized estate agents and a wealth of legal codes exist which facilitate pricing and transfer. Similar considerations exist for works of art and antiques. However in the latter case the actual goods transferred are individually differentiable, unlike transfers of shares or formal commodity exchange contracts; also information is less widely published and the buyer has less protection with respect to the quality of the product. Markets for personal skills are even more diffuse as to location of buyers and sellers, quality, price variability and terms of exchange. Evidently the availability of information, product standardization, merchantability due to many potential buyers and sellers, terms of exchange and pricing vary greatly with different classes of assets and services. In addition market characteristics such as the extent of monopolization, barriers to entry of new suppliers and exit of existing suppliers, the existence of substitute products, price regulation, fiscal effects etc complicate the valuation of non-security assets.

Alternative usage possibility as an influence upon asset values. Alternative usage possibility is a factor which affects the marketability of non-security assets; for example, land may be put to use for commercial, industrial, domestic or agricultural purposes, all of which have good marketability at most times. On the other hand special purpose machinery such as transfer lines for the motor industry or heavy horizontal borers for use in shipbuilding have very restricted marketability. To carry the example through, land may have a low current yield due to old controlled tenancies but high realizable value due to potential opportunity yields whereas a special purpose machine tool may have a current usage value much in excess of scrap realizable value. Alternative usage of land is relatively easy to value whereas the contribution to earning power of special purpose equipment would require specialist appraisal within the context of a particular manufacturing facility. Mobility of production resources either of plant components or of skilled labour is a further factor which affects marketability. Thus the important point is to recognize the conditioned basis of valuation of many assets; amongst other factors this may arise from product and industry dependence, location dependence or technological dependence. Possibly the most spectacular acquisition gains (and losses) are made when assets, in the broadest sense, are redeployed to alternative usages not envisaged by the seller.

If one accepts that it is only through redeployment or improvement in existing usage of resources that acquisitions can strictly benefit investors, given their opportunities for portfolio adjustment by exchange of shares, then one requisite for acquisition success is application of management skill to the combined resources superior to that which existed prior to the acquisition. Penrose (1966) suggests that company growth develops around certain skills and specialisms which are built up by employees. These skills might be exhibited in technological excellence, management reorganization ability, entrepreneurial opportunity seeking, fund raising and financing ability etc. Acquisitions provide a means of putting surplus skills to work profitably; therefore one would expect successful acquisitions to build upon specialist skills. From such a perspective it is clear that valuation of the potential target company is dependent upon the specialist skills and opportunities available to the acquirer. Assuming that such skills and opportunities are reflected in rates of return and growth prospects, their effects upon acquisition may be illustrated by a simple example involving one target company T and two bidder companies B_1 and B_2, for whom details are shown in Figure 2:10.

T is assumed to own a chain of cinemas with a potential infinite dividend paying capacity of £40 000 pa, a growth rate of 5% pa and a discount rate of 15% pa. B_1 is a property company and B_2 is a bingo hall group each of which could use the real assets of T with the ability to earn their respective rates of net dividend/net assets upon the value of T's net assets. All three companies own 20 equivalent sites.

Assuming that B_1 and B_2 bid for T solely in equity shares and aim to purchase T at £1 000 000, giving a bid premium of 20% over the dividend flow valuation, then B_1 could achieve additional capitalizable value of £1 333 000 for an outlay of £1 000 000 and B_2 could achieve additional capitalizable value of £1 667 000 for an outlay of £1 000000. Naturally the values depend upon the managements of B_1 and B_2 being able, and that of T unable, to achieve their respective ratio of dividends to site values of T. The example is highly simplistic and ignores uncertainties but is designed to indicate how rates of dividend, growth and discount can affect the possible acquisition valuations for a set of assets deployed to different uses. (It is not necessarily consistent with an equilibrium position in capital markets from a portfolio viewpoint.)

In the example, B_1 has the lowest discount rate which is intended to indicate that its earnings stream is the least risky of the three companies. On the other hand it has a lower growth rate of dividend flow than B_2 and a lower return from each site than either T or B_2. There can also be circumstances where it will pay an acquirer company to buy a company with a lower net cash flow/share than itself provided that the growth rate is somewhat higher. Various permutations of dividend payout, growth and discount rates are possible and may be examined in greater detail by reference to articles by Weston (1968) and by Silberman (1968). A further gross simplification in the example above is the assumption of infinite-dividend flows. In practical situations net cash inflows are generally discounted over some finite and proximate period, possibly 3 – 15 years depending on the type of acquisition and its growth and return prospects, and incorporate a terminal value figure for the company either on a break-up or a going-concern basis at the end of the period.

A further implicit assumption of the example is that there are adequate opportunities available to the companies B_1 and B_2 using T's sites to develop their respective property or bingo interests. This assumption serves for the example but is theoretically unreasonable since in general the marginal return to new investment projects will fall with the level of investment. The earnings stream which forms the basis of a decision by B_1 or B_2 is the additional earnings available discounted by the marginal rate of discount to shareholders whose portfolios contain shares in B_1 and B_2 respectively.

£000		Companies				
		T Cinemas	B_1	$[B_1 + T]$ Property	B_2	$[B_2 + T]$ Bingo
(1) No of sites:	pre-bid	20	20		20	
	post-bid			40		40
(2) Cash dividends (D) to share-holders net of tax pa		100	80	160	150	300
(3) Ratio (2)/(1)		5	4	4	7.5	7.5
(4) Growth rate of dividend pa (g)		0%	4%	4%	6%	6%
(5) Marginal discount rate (r)		12%	10%	10%	15%	15%
(6) Valuation* (V) of dividend flow		833	1 333	2 667	1 667	3 333

* Based upon infinite dividend flows using the formula $V = D/(r - g)$

Figure 2:10 Valuation of a target company by different acquirer companies

Exhibition of sources of risk in cash flow statistics. The discounted cash flow model for asset valuation which may, and in general should, always be used as a method of valuation of the marginal cash flows consequent upon a new project can incorporate riskiness of cash flows either by a simulation approach such as that advocated by Hertz (1964) or by more analytic forms where mathematical statistics are employed to summarize the effects of distributions of cash flows. Further refinements in analysis depend upon whether the analyst of the project is taking future cash flows as given or whether there exists discretion in that some form of optimization process is possible[8]. Exposition of techniques for such analysis is beyond the scope of this discussion; however it is worth making a conceptual point regarding the transfer of riskiness in underlying cash flows to a company into financial market measures of risk and return. In the latter case the returns to shareholders by way of share price change plus dividend flow can be well represented by the stable Paretian random walk model; in the former case the returns by way of net cash flows into the reserves of a company have not as yet been sufficiently researched to establish their statistical properties although evidence exists concerning the lack of correlation between (accruals) earnings of successive accounting periods. The evidence about the statistical nature of returns from individual non-security assets is almost non-existent. However, it is clear that a transformation process occurs between company capital investment risks, used here in terms of some suitable measure of variability such as variance or range of returns about a central measure such as the mean or median, and risks to investors by way of price movements in shares.

Intuitively it may be conjectured that the more varied is a company's product range, market diversification, supply sources and other regions of external dependency the more likely is its distribution of cash flow returns over a period of time to be near normal in form (by virtue of central limit theorem concepts). In the event that net cash flow returns over a period of time are regularly distributed in some well-known form such as the normal distribution, then the mean and variance statistics of cash flows will be useful parameters of cash flow profiles. In other cases, for example,if the histogram of cash flows over a period of time exhibits multiple peaks, then statistical categorization will be more complex. In contrast, companies with high exposure to one or two sources of external uncontrollable variability would tend to have earnings streams closely linked to the variability pattern of that source of risk; such variability may be highly non-normal and require appropriate statistical categorization. Thus it is important to consider sources of riskiness for assessing future cash flows from investment projects.

Diagrammatic clarification may help in emphasizing this point. One can envisage major one-off events which provide considerable risk such as nationalization, fire or explosion, or war, in which the effect is dramatic and of unknown duration. More familiar are fluctuations in economics often referred to as business cycles and shorter-term seasonal cycles. In the very short term small changes, often of unidentifiable cause, serve to add randomness to the business environment. Risk sources may be categorized with respect to a chosen time horizon and returns measured over intervals within that horizon. In a frequency sense important disturbances of long, medium and short term would be observed as peaks in Figure 2:11.

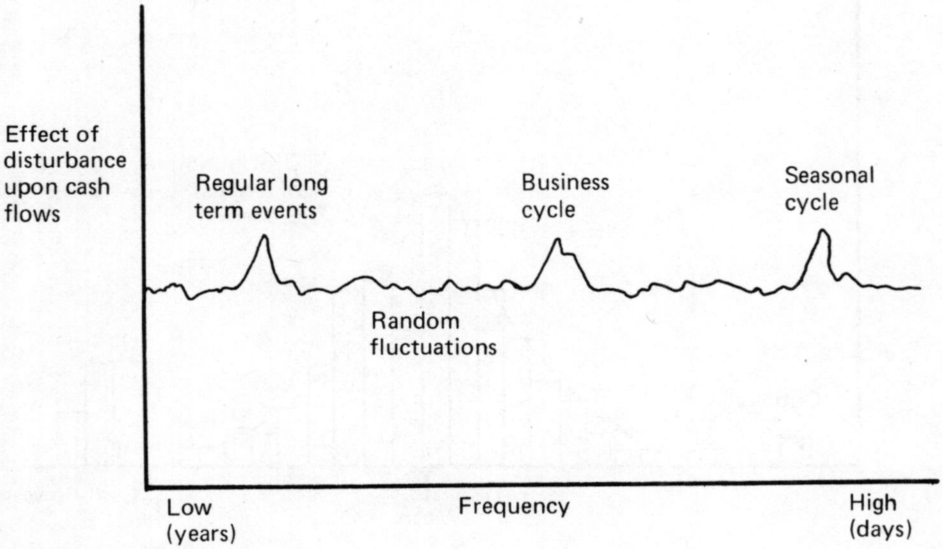

Figure 2:11 Identification of important frequency effects upon cash flows

Distributions of returns, analogous to Figure 2:2, measured at weekly intervals and with a horizon of, say, five years might produce a form as in Figure 2:12. This has the bulk of the movements in one region together with some outliers. These outliers should not be ignored just because they are irregular and in a sense unexpected given that expectations are mainly formed on the distribution of regular events. Possibly some analysts would wish to categorize the outliers illustrated in Figure 2:12 as the effects of (unquantifiable) uncertainty and the remaining regular distribution as the effect of (quantifiable) risk. Indeed it is the outliers which in terms of resulting cash flows are the most important in risk analysis. For a more theoretical treatment of these ideas the reader is referred to Mandelbrot (1969). Thus in drawing up distributions of cash flow returns from non-security assets for any particular time series or time period in the future, the lack of theory and empirical evidence complicates selection of either a theoretical or an empirical distribution. Either way the choice is a subjective judgment since the analyst makes an act of faith on persistence of prior period structure or on the shape and parameters of a theoretical distribution.

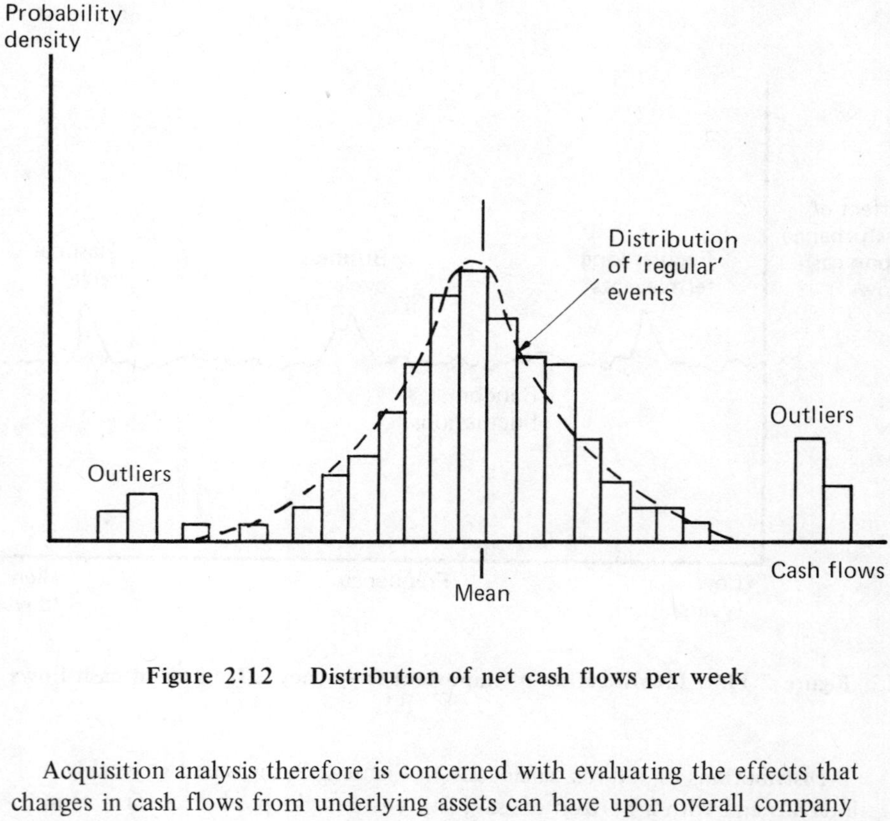

Figure 2:12 Distribution of net cash flows per week

Acquisition analysis therefore is concerned with evaluating the effects that changes in cash flows from underlying assets can have upon overall company valuation in security markets. The nature of such underlying assets is such that they frequently have multiple usage potential and therefore can be deployed with other assets in a variety of income-producing combinations. Distribution of cash flow returns from such assets is a matter of subjective judgment and in the assessment of risk the impact of potential sources of major but relatively unpredictable events should be considered.

Projection and analysis of acquisition returns

The preceding discussion suggests that acquisition investment appraisal should proceed with the following main aims:

1 Projection of net marginal cash flows attributable to acquirer company shareholders consequent upon the acquisition.
2 Projection of existing acquirer company cash flows as an independent company without the acquisition.
3 Assessment of relative riskiness of the future cash flow streams separately and together.
4 Assessment of the marginal net present value of the cash flows in (1) for given acquisition cost levels.

Whilst (1), (2) and (3) may raise difficulties in quantification of future cash flows and their distributions, (4) implies determination of the appropriate discount rate and assessment of the relative attractions of various financing plans. The latter can be investigated by making different projections for (1) and consequently (3) but the former would need to be estimated from historical data concerning the rating of the acquirer company in financial markets, in particular its systematic risk with respect to the market portfolios and mean return over some meaningful time period. These statistics can be estimated for the company and its industry based upon a historic set of stock prices and dividends for the company and indices (such as the FT Actuaries 500 Share Index and its relevant constituent industry indices). Estimation procedures using least-squares regression have been outlined by Blume (1970) for the general stable Paretian price distribution case, the objective being to estimate the parameters a and β in the market model (7), which is related to the earlier expressions (3) and (4),

$$R_j = a + \beta R_M + e \quad \text{for each time interval} \qquad (7)$$

where R_j is the observed return over the time interval for the jth share or industry

R_M is the observed return over the time interval for the market index

e is the error term over the time interval.

Using (5) and having obtained variance (R_M) as a result of estimating a and β above allows calculation of covariance (R_j, R_M) between the historic returns on the share and the market portfolio. The result of this may be interpreted as an approximate indication of the market standing of the acquirer shares from a portfolio viewpoint. This information could be readily monitored by a company interested in making acquisitions.

	Periods			
	1	2	3	4 . . N
Target company				
1 Disposals of assets	x	x	x	x . . x
2 Trading net cash flows	x	x	x	x . . x
3 Capital investments	x	x	x	x . . x
4 Financing flows (excl. 5)	x	x	x	x . . x
5 Cash flows from/to acquirer	x	x	x	x . . x
Total target company cash flows contingent upon acquisition	x	x	x	x . . x
Marginal cash flows available for dividend paying*	x	x	x	x . . x
Acquirer company				
Total cash flows independent of acquisition	x	x	x	x . . x

Statistics of cash flows

	Dividends to shareholders			
	Mean	Trend	Variance	Covariance
Target company Historic results				
Future projections (marginal above)*				
Acquirer company Historic results				
Future projections				

Statistics of security returns

	Historic	
	α	β
Target company		
Acquirer company		

Figure 2:13 Acquisition cash flow projections

Simulation approach to cash flow projections. The procedure for assembling cash flow projections in corporate valuation models has been extensively described elsewhere[9] so that only a summarized format is shown here. The projection of cash flows responsive to (1) above may be assembled as illustrated in Figure 2:13 in headings concerned with disposals of assets, continued trading activities, capital investments, acquisition-financing flows and effects upon acquirer-company cash flows. The last-mentioned caption should take up any effects upon the cash flows which the acquirer company may otherwise expect in the absence of the acquisition, for example the need to provide short-term cash finance. The cash flow projections under (2) are self-explanatory and would come from budgetary procedures.

Statistics of historic and future cash flows are designed to assist evaluation of growth and riskiness in cash flow streams of both the companies pre- and post-acquisition. Evidently if each future period cash flow is a probabilistic measure, the statistics of cash flows themselves will be probabilistic. Care should be taken to project like with like for the two companies; in other words if both companies are affected by the same economic fluctuations it would be incorrect to calculate covariances of cash flows which imply different values for the same underlying economic circumstances. To clarify, let vectors $\mathbf{v}$ and $\mathbf{u}$ contain elements 1 to N for total cash flows of the target and acquirer companies respectively and let n simulations be made for a different set of economic circumstances. The n sets of period cash flows may be included in matrices $\mathbf{V}$ and $\mathbf{U}$ in Figure 2:14. It would be inappropriate to calculate covariances of $\mathbf{u}$ and $\mathbf{v}$ vectors except those of $\mathbf{u}$ and $\mathbf{v}$ in respect of similar underlying projection circumstances. Thus simulation run 2 for the target company which generates $\mathbf{v}_2$ and run 2 for the acquirer company which generates $\mathbf{u}_2$ should have consistent underlying growth rates etc to yield a meaningful covariance between $\mathbf{v}_2$ and $\mathbf{u}_2$

Computer-based models make analysis such as this perfectly feasible, while a less detailed indicative analysis can be carried out by taking three or four possible circumstances for manual projections as in Figure 2:13. Unless the two companies are in very different businesses and/or economies then it is unlikely that covariance will alter greatly with respect to different simulation runs; the covariance measure in its portfolio context is essentially a time-series concept rather than a net-present-value concept.

The cash flow statistics mean and trend give some indications of past cash flow average return and growth; one could separate out trading and capital movements for each period. The level and variability of cash flows per share, especially trading net cash flows, may be compared with the market model parameters a and β as an indication of the historic response of investors to the stream of trading cash flows. Unfortunately there is a lack of detailed studies designed to clarify the extent of these relationships. Indeed they may remain somewhat clouded until the quality of reported accounting data improves. However such information would allow the analyst to form (subjective) judgments about the response of investors to realization of future earnings-stream projections. If for example the target company has a lower systematic risk (with respect to the market portfolio) than the acquirer and the covariance between acquirer and target-projected earnings streams is low then the combined earnings streams would have high defensive quality. The ultimate capitalization will depend upon the joint risk-and-return position on Figure 2:7 with respect to the efficient frontier and efficiency of the security market. Movements as a result of the acquisition to the right and/or downwards would cause the combined capitalization to be reduced whereas movements to the left and/or upwards would cause investors to bid up prices. Ideally comparison of historic pre-acquisition relative states of the combining companies with projected post-acquisition state of the combined companies should indicate an increase in trend, a reduced covariance and a higher mean (expectation) of cash flows.

It should be stressed that although the foregoing analytic framework is only suggestive it is founded upon accepted theoretical constructs and empirical evidence such as tests of efficiency of security markets discussed in earlier sections. Evidence presented in subsequent chapters concerning acquisition activity tends to support the relevance of such a framework for acquisition appraisal.

Matrix **V**

Simulations	Periods 1	2	3	N
1	v_{11}	v_{12}	v_{13}	v_{1N}
2				
3				
.				
.				
.				
n	v_{n1}	v_{n2}	v_{n3}	v_{nN}

Matrix **U**

Simulations	Periods 1	2	3	N
1	u_{11}	u_{12}	u_{13}	u_{1N}
2				
3				
.				
.				
.				
n	u_{n1}	u_{n2}	u_{n3}	u_{nN}

Figure 2:14 Matrices of cash flow projections from simulation runs

'Cost of Capital' measures for acquisition appraisal

A great deal of discussion has arisen over questions surrounding a company's cost of capital – whether a firm's overall cost of capital depends at all upon its capital structure debt-to-equity ratio – how to measure cost of capital – how to integrate capital budgeting concepts of returns to investment into portfolio valuation models – what criteria to use in capital budgeting decisions for investment selection. Without aiming to be drawn into each of these topics in detail it is relevant to indicate the nature of the various controversies and attempt to draw out a set of consistent concepts which may be used in acquisition analysis.

Some issues concerning cost of capital. The first topic has been widely discussed and originated with papers by Modigliani and Miller (1958), (1963), (1966), who suggested that, in perfectly competitive capital markets without transaction costs or taxes and where all investors are rational profit maximizers, any two sets of assets which offer identical returns in terms of quantity and quality (riskiness) will have the same value irrespective of the way they are financed. Thus a set of assets financed 100% by debt would have the same value as if they were financed 100% by equity. Investors can create their own gearing by borrowings at the personal level so that company gearing is irrelevant. Traditional theories of company financing assume that there is some best balance between debt and equity finance for a particular quality of earnings stream at which the company is most highly valued by investors, and thus its cost of capital overall is minimized. In fact once the tax effect of debt-interest allowances against corporate tax is included in the Modigliani and Miller argument and adjustment is made for various personal borrowing restrictions on investors and legal limitations of transfer between debt and equity markets, the practical difference vanishes between their model and that of the traditional theory of finance. Discussion of the differences between the two theories is well set out in Solomon (1963). The overall conclusion for practical financial management is that the costs of various kinds of capital finance in relation to debt-to-equity levels takes the form of Figure 2:15. This allows for a minimal overall cost of capital and a corresponding maximum valuation for the firm at some intermediate ratio of debt to equity. This point will vary significantly from company to company: for example, property companies are traditionally highly geared in comparison with engineering companies presumably because loan stock holders consider the earnings stream available from property assets to be a much less risky cover for their interest payments than earnings from traditionally volatile engineering activities. Consequently an acquisition strategy should aim to create a post-acquisition financial structure which is close to perceived optimal levels for the type of company. In practical terms this is likely to be phrased in terms of achieving a financial structure which is not so high as to create an unusual degree of risk for fixed-interest stockholders nor so low as to neglect the tax advantages of debt finance. Constraints on these levels are discussed more fully in the next chapter.

The other questions concerning cost of capital are largely interrelated. If it is accepted that changes in a company's investments, as a result of either internal or external investment, affect its attractions to investor portfolios then capital-budgeting decisions must be seen as an adjustment to both financing and investment decisions. Consequently selection of the best acquisition plan becomes no less than optimization of the whole firm over some suitable time horizon and within feasible constraints such as available finance etc.

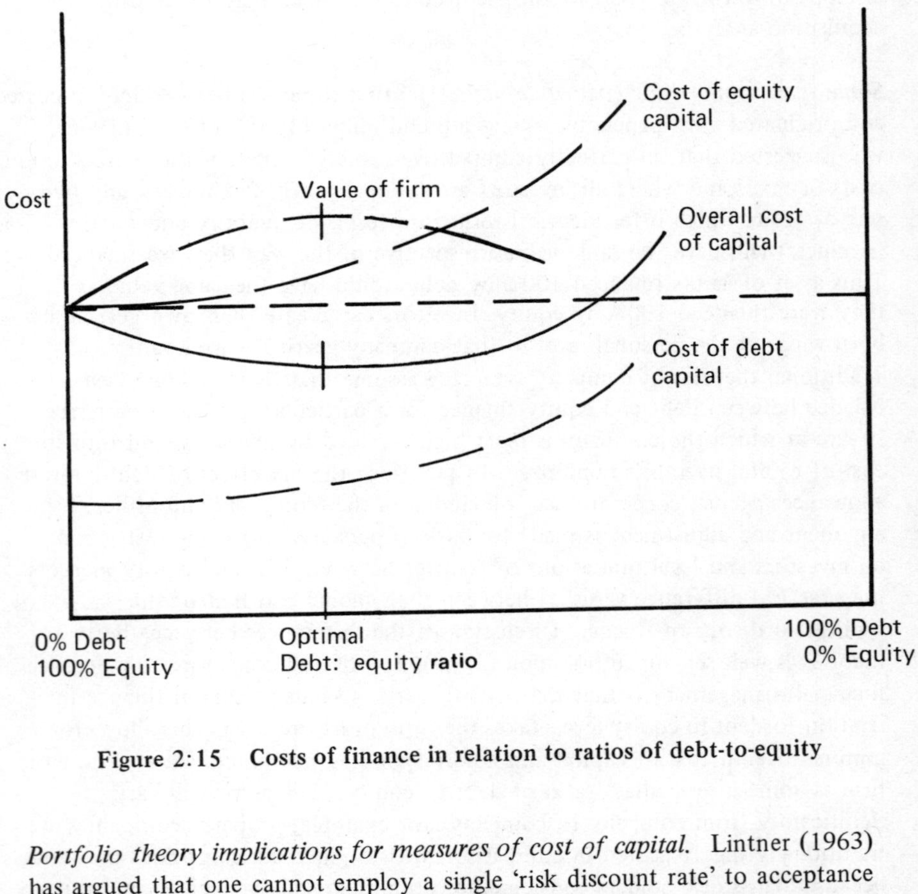

Figure 2:15 Costs of finance in relation to ratios of debt-to-equity

Portfolio theory implications for measures of cost of capital. Lintner (1963) has argued that one cannot employ a single 'risk discount rate' to acceptance or rejection decisions between different individual projects out of a choice of projects since each one has a different interplay of variance and covariance with existing portfolios held by individual investors. Following this argument and making the assumption that investors hold well-diversified portfolios similar to the market portfolio mentioned earlier, the acquisition strategist should aim to assess the marginal impact of a proposed acquisition upon the market portfolio to which the security return statistics of Figure 2:13 relate.

The form of the analysis would consider the effect of company X acquiring company Y with different financing instruments or combinations of them. Cash consideration would cause investors in Y to receive a risk-free asset; loans or equity consideration would give investors in Y a risky asset. Investors therefore change from holding the market portfolio to a new portfolio, being the market portfolio less holdings in Y plus some combination of a holding in X, a holding in loan stock of X and a holding of risk-free cash. The change in portfolio implies a change in overall portfolio variance with respect to the changes in X and Y together. For a maintained expected return pre- and post-acquisition a reduced overall variance would be sought. The selection of optimal financing instruments for the change in X is independent of the change in Y, ie Y is taken over as a precondition of a change in investors' holdings of X's securities. Thus the problem which is to be solved is not what acquisition gives the highest net present value or rate of return over some cut-off level but rather what acquisition and financing package most benefits portfolio investors. The absolute rate of discount or cost of capital is largely a non-issue to the analysis which is concerned with relative portfolio changes.

Unfortunately the difficulty of taking decisions based upon marginal advantage to portfolios is as complex as trying to locate cost of capital levels for specific risk classes. In a theoretical analysis of the interdependence of corporate retentions, growth rate of profits and variability of profits, Lintner (1964) has shown that the appropriate cut-off rate for new investments within a capital budget is substantially in excess of the current earnings yield of a company and is directly proportional to the retention rate (or size of capital budget assuming retained funds are reinvested), the variability of future returns both within capital-budget cash flows and in share price volatility, and the growth rate of the company's earnings stream. Lintner's analysis is largely of long-run relevance but serves to show that most accepted methods of calculating marginal 'cost of capital' are likely to underestimate the true investment cut-off rate primarily due to compounded effects of riskiness in future returns. It also suggests that increasing relative size of target to acquirer company, ie a larger (acquisition) capital budget, may be expected to require relatively greater expectations of return.

Appendix 1 indicates the portfolio framework within which investors in target and acquirer company shares would evaluate a change in their portfolio risk-return characteristics. The analysis is simplified to the somewhat restricted two-security case but serves to show that the variables involved include the size of investment holdings, expected returns, variability of returns, and covariances between security returns within the portfolios. In practice the cases which are likely to present problems of analysis arise when the returns on one of the combining stocks are negatively correlated with either the other combining company or the remainder of an investor's portfolio.

The framework of Figure 2:13 is designed to indicate whether the profile of returns and the covariance of the combining company returns either together or individually in conjunction with a stock market index, which should approximate to the market portfolio concept, change radically as a result of the acquisition. This would be indicated if either the covariance between historic results and future projections changed sign in the tableau for 'statistics of cash flows' or if one of the β coefficients in the tableau for 'statistics of security returns' was statistically less than unity or negative. Otherwise and in general it may be presumed that increased return for similar variance or decreased variance for similar returns or a combination of increased returns and decreased variance as a result of acquisition will be advantageous to shareholders.

The incremental cash flows to shareholders in the acquirer company arise from that part of the total target company's cash flows contingent upon acquisition which may be attributed to dividend paying. Capital maintaining investment is a prior deduction in arriving at this marginal cash flow available for dividends. A marginal terminal value should be included in year N if cash flows are not projected to infinity. Comparison of the trend and variance measures of past and projected dividend flows provide direct measures of the changes in returns to shareholders, excluding overall stock market price fluctuations.

Notes

1 See for example Granger and Morgenstern (1970), Chapter 6. However 'randomness' has been probed, so far as stock price movements are concerned only to the extent of the distribution of price changes, correlations between sequences of price changes, filter rules and runs up and down. It is still quite possible that predictable behaviour exists although it is clearly hard to locate.

2 Readers who wish to familiarize themselves with the mathematics of stable Paretian models should refer to papers by Fama and Roll (1968), (1971).

3 Granger and Morgenstern (1970), Chapter 3 discuss the random walk model in detail. Readers may also find Fama (1970) useful as a survey article on capital markets.

4 Friend and Puckett (1964) discuss dividends, growth and stock price relationships. Rayner and Little (1966) suggest that there is no correlation between past and future earnings growth.

5 M.D. Fitzgerald's work at Manchester Business School indicates that brokers' circulars promote response in share prices to reflect bullish or bearish information contained in the circular.

6 The simulation studies by Clarkson (1962) in the small and Orcutt *et al.* (1961) in the large, although compiled from aggregation of behaviour in the small, could provide leads to an approach to market simulation.

7 See for example Merrett and Sykes (1963) and the book by Lawson and Bean (1975) on corporate valuation by discounted cash flow analysis.

8 Typically analysts would try to seek a linear approximation to the problem so that linear programming methods can be used or if this is an inappropriate technique in the circumstances then recourse must be had to non-linear techniques assuming that a suitable method exists which will enable a solution to be reached.

9 See note 7 above.

3

Financial Market Constraints

Introduction

No financial analyst would claim that the practical circumstances in which business is conducted correspond exactly with those assumed in the literature of business finance; the latter naturally has to abstract from detail and develop the interactions of those influences which appear to be the most important. It is usually assumed for example that all investors in financial markets are equally well informed, that security markets are perfectly competitive and free of transaction costs and that riskiness can be characterized in statistical terms. The usefulness of such assumptions for explanation of aggregate 'macro'-behaviour is supported by the good correspondence between theoretical constructs and the results of many empirical studies into portfolio investment practice, randomness of stock market prices and discounting of information in share prices. However at the 'micro'-level of decision-making by individual investors or individual companies it is well recognized both by theoreticians and by practitioners that deviation of behaviour in the small from aggregated patterns may be extensive. For example the separation of management from ownership tends to produce a transfer of profit to managers at the expense of shareholders and a reduction in the extent of shareholder wealth maximizing behaviour[1]. Clearly transaction costs are involved in the trading of stocks and shares. Banks take fees and underwriting commissions on new issues of securities. Information is more extensively sought by institutional investors than by individuals. Some future events cannot readily be included in the concept of risk and remain as unquantifiable and often unknowable contingencies which are generally referred to as uncertainty; the distinction is made clearly in Farrar (1967).

As a framework for the understanding of general financial behaviour, the continuing usefulness of theoretical constructs is not in doubt but at a practical micro-level of decisiong-making one may expect 'rules of thumb' and 'accepted practices' to be more familiar reference points than ideas of optimization of theoretically derived models. Partly this reflects the fact that the extension of theory-based models of (financial) behaviour to include detailed aspects of the real business environment often renders such models extremely complex and/or unpractical to use for time-constrained decision-making. Furthermore the time lag between research and the reporting of empirical results to test explanatory theories tends to be a matter of years so that rules of thumb are requisites for business survival whereas theories do not have such practical necessity! Nevertheless, as in most branches of science, business practice, theory and innovation are in continuing step so that there is a need to explain existing phenomena, test such explanations against real business activity and innovate, both as a result of practice and as a result of theoretical developments. The fact that theoretical assumptions are not perfectly realized in practice should not deter either practitioners from debating the value of the theory nor theoreticians from suggesting potential improvements to practice. In such a dialogue there is an important need to relate theoretical ideas and decision methods to those rules of thumb and conventions adopted in the actual business environment. This is a prime objective in the subsequent discussion concerning financial market constraints and their importance regarding financial strategy for acquisitions.

Financially-oriented acquirer companies

The analysis begins by examining how acquisition activity has occurred in relation to fluctuations in the stock market during recent years and then narrows down to examine the financing of acquisitions in which the objectives most closely approximate to maximization of shareholder net present wealth. Since evidence concerning actual acquisitions by such companies forms an important component of the discussion it is worth commenting briefly upon the sources of data and research methods.

Research methods outlined. There have been a number of econometric studies which examine the financial aspects of acquisitions in general, for example to investigate whether acquisitions achieve economies of scale or whether one can identify certain types of companies which are likely to be taken over[2], but few which examine case studies of acquisitions or focus upon objectives of acquirer executives. The study of Newbould (1970) of merger activity amongst UK quoted companies during the mid-sixties emphasized the range of managerial objectives in merger activity but did not attempt to categorize these objectives in relation to identifiable company groups. Since the emphasis of this monograph is upon financial strategy it was decided to try to segregate companies which achieved growth primarily by financial reorganization and rationalization of companies acquired from other companies, namely those which did not rely upon acquisition as a means of growth or which pursued an active acquisition policy largely with a view to industrial product and factor market position adjustment rather than financial reorganization. The group of companies which pursued growth by acquisition and financial reorganization was then examined in greater detail, especially by interviews with executives in those companies and by case studies based purely upon publicly available information such as press comment, annual reports and offer documents.

In essence the questions posed in the research were:

1 Is there a category of acquirer company, defined as 'financially-oriented', which can be seen as different from other acquirers? If so what are the distinguishing features?
2 How significant in terms of total merger and acquisition activity amongst UK publicly quoted companies is the financially-oriented category?
3 What institutional constraints of a financial nature exist upon the activities of financially-oriented acquirer companies?
4 How do such companies operate?
5 What implications does this have for the application of existing bodies of knowledge to the acquisition activities of the companies which tend to be regarded as financially-oriented?
6 What implications does financially-oriented acquisition activity have for companies engaged in other acquisitions, eg for adjustment of product and factor market positions?

Segregation of a financially-oriented (F-type) group of acquirer companies from other companies presented a problem in that definition of the criteria for financial orientation in advance of classification would have made results derived from detailed analysis somewhat tautological. Consequently reference was made to a number of experts in acquisition activity to assess whether they regarded certain types of acquisitions to be motivated by financial rather than product or factor market adjustment considerations and, assuming they agreed with such a distinction, to request a classification of companies in the F-type category. Details of the research process may be found elsewhere[3]; the F-type classification indicated wide agreement amongst the experts – including stockbrokers, merchant bankers, financial journalists, and executives of acquirer companies – as to which companies were regarded as financially-oriented. A list of the financially-oriented group is given in Appendix 2.

Behavioural approach. It was decided to pursue a research approach (for fuller details of which see Appendix 5) using interviews and case studies to investigate the behaviour of F-type acquirer companies. The decision was based upon the following considerations:

1 Since prior research in depth on such a group of companies was not extensive, it appeared relevant to gather data on a variety of topics both qualitative as well as quantitative.
2 Interviews would yield valuable unanticipated data which would not otherwise be available. The interviews could be framed around questionnaires designed both to gather data systematically and to stimulate discussion.
3 Case studies could be used in conjunction with interview results as a check on the interview data.
4 Interview and case study data are prerequisites upon which later models may be built for more statistically-oriented research studies.

The emphasis of the research was on learning about financially-oriented acquisition activity in its variety rather than on testing a specific aggregated model of such activity. In fact the research procedure was a multi-stage process which adopted the following sequence.

1 Survey of literature concerning acquisitions in general.
2 Interviews with a variety of experts involved in acquisition activity and assessment of the relevance of separately classifying F-type acquirer companies.
3 Construction of a hypothetical model of F-type acquirer company behaviour and associated interview questionnaire.
4 Second interviews with experts to achieve a classification of F-type acquirers and to obtain questionnaire responses.
5 Analysis of case studies of two acquirer companies in depth over a sequence of acquisitions.
6 Integration of case study and interview results to refine the model and discuss the results in relation to the literature.

A full rationale for the research design and the methods of analysing the interview and case study results may be found in the author's PhD thesis, Manchester Business School, 1973.

Explanation based upon a 'satisficing' model

Decision-makers faced with problems which they must solve will generally find that there is a variety of possible solutions, some of which are clearly more preferable than others and others which are less obvious to distinguish preferentially. Optimal solutions to some problems may be obtained by a suitable analytical technique, eg linear or dynamic programming, or in complex non-linear or stochastic problems possibly by the use of simulation methods. However it is relevant to ask whether, even if one can fully specify the problem in mathematical terms, it is worth the cost and/or time of detailed analysis to reach optimal solutions. In many cases time is a critical limit on the amount of analysis that can be made prior to reaching a decision; this is particularly so in the case of acquisition decisions. Frequently either one cannot fully specify a problem in quantitative terms or the qualitative factors are dominant to the decision. Whilst one may conceive of an idealized optimal solution to a particular problem, the feasibility of reaching such an optimum depends on being able to fully specify the problem, locate a method appropriate to obtaining an optimal solution, carry out the necessary steps in a given time, and interpret the results into a decision strategy.

In some business circumstances optimization methods have received widespread acceptance, for example the application of linear programming to oil-refinery operations, critical-path scheduling to construction projects and statistical-decision theory to mineral exploration. In most circumstances either the problem has to be simplified so far that the concept of optimality becomes very restricted in the context of the real problem or sub-optimal solutions are sought either intuitively or as a conscious cost-effective choice.

As soon as there is an interest in explaining the adaptive behaviour of companies at the individual level then micro-economic theory of the firm is not the appropriate reference theory. Clearly acquisition activity is a particularly good example of adaptive behaviour in that significant changes in the states of both combining companies result from an acquisition. Explanation of acquisition activity needs to look to a theoretical framework which allows for adaptive behaviour. Since no extensive theory specific to acquisition activity exists it was an objective of the research to contribute ideas concerning the financial considerations in acquisition activity which might assist the development of such a theory. Therefore 'satisficing' concepts of goals, aspiration levels and constraints were used as the framework within which acquisition activity was analysed on the grounds that adaptive behaviour and decision-making under limited information can be best incorporated into such a framework.

The idea that businessmen 'satisfice' has received considerable attention in the academic literature, especially that of organizational theory. On this argument businessmen set 'goals' that they wish to achieve and associate 'aspiration levels' with these respective goals. Aspiration levels rise or fall over a period of time as experience indicates the degree of ease or difficulty in achieving them. Constraints in the business environment limit the feasible solutions to goals; furthermore decision-makers collect only a limited amount of information consistent with available cost and time. Decision-making is therefore seen as a process of reaching a good decision on a rational basis which is constrained by available information and real or perceived constraints upon possible solutions[4]. Marris (1966) in particular has extended these ideas to develop a behavioural model of acquisition raiders, analogous in many respects to the F-type acquirers of this study, and Penrose (1966) has proposed a theory of general corporate growth which is consistent with 'satisficing' concepts.

Penrose suggests that companies specialize in particular activities and build up strong operating bases within specializations from which the company can expand and adapt. Since firms are rarely able to employ their resources fully at any one instant, imbalances in resource utilization build up and ultimately force a need and opportunity for growth. Resources are widely defined to include plant, equipment, materials, human resources and finance. This is an adaptive model of corporate growth rather than one which conforms to classical economic concepts of optimizing profit in particular static market conditions. Indeed the focus of classical economic theory of the firm is not so much upon decision-making within particular firms but rather upon the behaviour of firms in general in the market place.

Macro-context of acquisition activity

It has been suggested that acquisition activity coincides with stock market price movements[5] in that activity rises during a bull market and declines during a bear market. This notion was investigated using data for the Financial Times All-Share Index and for the number and value of acquisitions involving UK quoted companies. The data is shown in Figure 3:1 and covers a full stock market cycle from the third quarter peak of 1968 to the first-quarter peak of 1972. It includes data for the total number of bids and deals involving quoted companies and also data for the financially-oriented subset of companies listed in Appendix 2.

The model which was tested took the form

$$N_t = a + bF_t + c(F_t - F_{t-1}) + e_t$$

where t = time

N = number or value measures of bids

F = level of the Financial Times All-Share Index

a, b, c are the parameters of the model

e = disturbance term

Tests using this model were made to investigate the association of overall acquisition activity with Stock Exchange index levels and also to investigate the average bid size of both overall and F-type bids in relation to Stock Exchange index levels.

Test 1. Overall acquisition activity in relation to FT All-Share Index. The following data series were used for N and results are shown in Figure 3:2. For each series the model was estimated with and without the change in stock price variable. Estimation was by ordinary least-squares regression.

The results in terms of $\bar{R}^2$ are not of great importance, rather the objective is to look at the significance of the b and c coefficients in the different models.

Figure 3:1 Quarterly data of acquisition activity involving UK publicly quoted companies

Quarter	F-type acquirers (1)		Total (2)		A/C %	B/D %	Average bid size		(3)
	A Number	B Value £m	C Number	D Value £m			'F-type' B/A £m	Total D/C £m	FT All-share Index
1968/4	6	48.3	82	728.1	7.3	6.5	8.1	8.9	164.8
1969/1	4	54.8	107	1 130.9	3.7	4.9	13.6	9.6	170.5
2	3	5.1	67	282.4	4.5	1.8	1.7	4.2	151.5
3	4	9.5	58	297.1	6.9	3.2	2.4	5.1	137.3
4	6	17.1	64	486.1	9.4	3.5	2.9	7.6	139.1
1970/1	8	23.4	72	557.8	11.1	4.2	2.9	7.7	146.5
2	7	11.6	65	243.0	10.8	4.8	1.7	3.7	128.6
3	5	10.6	63	258.3	7.9	4.1	2.1	4.1	129.2
4	4	11.5	46	148.3	8.7	7.7	2.9	3.2	135.8
1971/1	10	21.1	51	135.7	19.6	15.6	2.1	2.7	135.8
2	14	41.3	72	294.5	19.5	14.1	2.9	4.1	156.5
3	13	34.0	77	461.2	16.9	7.4	2.6	6.0	180.1
4	16	55.4	91	826.4	17.6	6.7	3.5	9.1	181.6
1972/1	10	98.2	87	1 399.2	11.5	7.0	9.8	16.1	205.9

Notes: 1 The identification of F-type companies is described in the text. By 1972 there were approximately 40 such companies. The number and value of their bids is taken from the Financial Times weekly Saturday report of bids and deals amongst UK publicly quoted companies.

2 The data is the quarterly sum of the number and value of bids reported in the Financial Times weekly Saturday report of bids and deals involving UK publicly quoted companies.

3 The FT All-Share Index is the average of monthly data given in *Financial Statistics*, HMSO, London.

Regression number	Dependent variable	Constant a	Independent variable coefficients b	Independent variable coefficients c	$\bar{R}^2$	D
1.1	N_1	−127.0 (30.6)	1.10 (0.196)		0.41	1.42
1.2	N_1	−116.0 (33.4)	1.02 (0.216)	0.63 (0.73)	0.41	1.38
2.1	N_2	−1.09 (1.50)	0.0429 (0.0096)		0.31	1.94
2.2	N_2	−1.78 (1.63)	0.0477 (0.011)	−0.039 (0.036)	0.31	2.00
3.1	N_3	−0.203 (0.75)	0.0127 (0.0048)		0.12	1.83
3.2	N_3	−0.89 (0.78)	0.0174 (0.0050)	−0.038 (0.017)	0.20	1.98
4.1	N_4	−0.20 (0.68)	0.0111 (0.0044)		0.12	1.17
4.2	N_4	−0.96 (0.69)	0.0164 (0.0044)	−0.043 (0.015)	0.24	2.06

Notes: The figures in brackets are the standard errors of the coefficients

$\bar{R}^2$ is the multiple correlation coefficient adjusted for degrees of freedom

D is the Durbin-Watson statistic

N_1 is the total value of bids and deals

N_2 is the total number of bids and deals

N_3 is the number of bids and deals offering cash or a cash alternative

N_4 is as for N_3 but excluding bids made by foreign or unincorporated bidders

Figure 3:2 Acquisition activity for all acquisitions: regression results

In all the regressions the b coefficient is significant at the 1% level. In regressions which include the first difference of the FT Actuaries All-Share Index as well as its level, the first difference is only significant for the number of cash bids as shown by regressions 3.2 and 4.2. In both these cases the c coefficient has a negative sign and is significant at the 2.5% level. (The Durbin-Watson statistics in regressions 1.1, 1.2 and 4.1 are sufficiently low to suggest that autocorrelation may be present in these equations.)

These results suggest that over the data period the incidence of bids and deals measured by value and number were significantly correlated with the Stock Exchange index level. A further implication arises from the significance of the c coefficients for cash bids and their negative signs; this suggests that cash is used more frequently during periods when the stock market is falling and less frequently when the stock market is rising. The sign of the constant terms is negative in all equations which suggests that there is a minimum level of the index below which bids and deals would not occur, ie a minimum capitalization level of companies in general. However if the index were to fall that low there is no guarantee that the mechanisms of bids and deals would be the same as at present. Furthermore only for regressions 1.1 and 1.2 is the constant term more than twice its standard error.

Test 2. Average bid size in relation to FT All-Share Index. Bids by those companies which were classified as F-type acquirer companies were segregated from the overall data of acquisition activity. The number and value of F-type bids over the period studied are shown in columns A and B of Figure 3:1. The increasing significance of F-type bids in relation to the total number and value of acquisitions may be seen from the ratios of columns A:C and B:D . The data for F-type acquirer bids in quarters 1968/4, 1969/1 and 1972/1 were influenced by one unusually large bid in each case; however, exclusion of the particular bid would not alter the direction of change between quarters.

The stock market capitalization of companies in total provides the basis for calculating share price indices such as the FT All-Share Index. Consequently if there are limits on the relative sizes of bidder and target companies measured in terms of equity capitalization then average bid size may be expected to vary roughly in line with stock market indices. Accordingly a regression was made of bid sizes against the FT All-Share Index in a similar manner to Test 1. The models tested were:

$$\text{(A)} \quad N_t = a + bF_t + c(F_t - F_{t-1}) + e_t$$

$$\text{(B)} \quad \log N_t = a + b \log F_t + e_t$$

where the symbols are the same as for Test 1 except that the two series for N , N_1 and N_2 relate respectively to total bids and to bids made by F-type acquirer companies.

Model (B) was thought to be the more realistic on the grounds that proportionate changes would be more closely correlated than absolute changes, especially if bidders were attempting to maximize the size of the target company. Model (A) was fitted both including and excluding the change in share index variable. Results of ordinary least-squares regression are shown in Figure 3:3.

	Regression number	Dependent variable	Constant a	Independent variable coefficients		$\bar{R}^2$	D
				b	c		
Model (A)	1.1	N_1	−13.05 (4.02)	0.127 (0.026)		0.64	0.98
	1.2	N_1	−14.21 (5.20)	0.135 (0.034)	−0.022 (0.058)	0.61	1.11
	2.1	N_2	−10.44 (5.54)	0.095 (0.036)		0.32	1.48
	2.2	N_2	−11.14 (7.20)	0.100 (0.047)	−0.013 (0.080)	0.26	1.55
Model (B)	3.1	$\log N_1$	−5.20 (1.39)	2.73 (0.634)		0.57	0.88
	4.1	$\log N_2$	−6.15 (2.08)	3.06 (0.954)		0.42	1.54

The figures in brackets are the standard errors of the coefficients

$\bar{R}^2$ and D are as for Test 1

Figure 3:3 Average bid sizes: regression results

The constant terms are mostly significant at the 5% level and again had negative signs which may be interpreted similarly to the results of Test 1. The c coefficients were not significant in either of the regressions 1.2 and 2.2 indicating that there is little association between bid size and rate of change of the index. However this should be interpreted cautiously as rate of change of the index introduces an autocorrelation term into the regression equation, and in none of the regressions do the Durbin-Watson statistics justify the conclusion that autocorrelation is absent from the equations as specified.

More important are the significance and value of the b coefficients. They were significant at the 1% level for regressions 1.1, 1.2, 3.1, 4.1 at the 5% level for regression 2.1, and at the 10% for regression 2.2. The relatively low $\overline{R}^2$ statistics indicate that the explanatory power of the equations is weak although as with Test 1 the object was not to achieve a high degree of goodness of fit but rather to examine the significance of the b coefficients.

Over the same period the average size of bids in total and by F-type acquirers was significantly correlated with the absolute level of the FT All-Share Index but was not correlated with changes in the Index. From Model (B) it appears that a 1% change in the level of the Index is associated with an approximate 3% change in the average bid size. Model (B) was inferior to Model (A) for the overall acquisition data but superior for the F-type acquisition data. The question of a size constraint in terms of the relative equity market capitalization of bidder and target firms is discussed subsequently but a possible explanation for the better fit of Model (B) than Model (A) to F-type acquirers lies in the fact that prior acquisitions boost the capitalization base for the next acquisition so that growth in equity capitalization can approach a geometric expansion. The data for acquirers in total includes bids by companies which are not growing primarily by acquisition.

Overall one can conclude that acquisition activity over the data period was correlated with the level of the stock market. Possible reasons for such a correlation, which would require further research to prove or disprove, include the following:

1 Equity consideration is more acceptable to target company shareholders in periods of bullish than in periods of bearish markets.
2 Liquidity available to finance acquisitions is correlated with rising stock markets.
3 Both acquirer and acquired firms' shareholders can see profitable opportunities from acquisitions made on a rising market.

The significance of F-type acquirers may be noted in that less than 40 companies accounted for between 5 and 20% of all bids amongst quoted companies.

Funding constraints

The theory of portfolio investment, discussed earlier, implies risk diversification in financial markets and that acquirer company executives should seek to increase return and/or decrease risk for investors in the shares of the company. The advantages of debt in company capital structure up to some level has also been mentioned. In theory one could specify a maximization problem which aims to maximize the portfolio advantage of a particular capital structure, or in possibly more familiar terms minimize cost of capital for a capital structure mix. Adoption of a 'satisficing' approach suggests that constraints may be specified regarding debt:equity levels. In practice one finds that issue terms of loan stocks limit the level of company borrowings in relation to net tangible assets and interest on debt in relation to company earnings. This suggests that two constraints can be specified, one for debt:net tangible assets or equity and one for interest cover out of earnings. These are normally referred to as 'net tangibles' and 'times interest' covers.

Acquisition size. Early interviews with experts in acquisition activity suggested that acquisitions of a size, measured by equity market capitalization, much greater than that of the acquirer company would tend to be frowned upon by institutional investors unless the bid was framed as a reverse bid, eg where the larger company in fact acquires the smaller but the management of the smaller company ends up in control of the combined companies. Reasons for institutional disapproval of acquisitions much larger in size than the acquirer were related to confidence in the ability of the acquirer company management to handle the combined companies successfully. There was a general feeling that a track record of successful acquisitions, which yielded rising assets and earnings per share, would increase such confidence. Consequently a third constraint was hypothesized based upon the relative size of the target to the acquirer company.

Net tangible assets and earnings per share. All the experts agreed that acquisition objectives could be defined in terms of growth in net tangible assets and earnings per share, these being measured in accrual accounting terms as disclosed in company accounts but adjusted for revaluations of property assets, in particular, to near-realizable values. Two further constraints were hypothesized to reflect these objectives based upon dilution of assets per share and dilution of earnings per share consequent upon an acquisition. Both were defined in terms of latest earnings information available to investors, ie most recent results or forecasts for the current year in cases where forecasts had been made. These measures may be interpreted as information which portfolio investors use to form their expectations of returns to shareholdings and which becomes discounted in share prices thereby yielding actual returns to investors by way of share price movements. Experts regarded asset backing for a share price as a contributory factor to risk reduction in that shareholders have an ultimate stop on potential losses by way of realizable value. However the value of this stop could only occur by way of a bid since insolvency and consequent liquidation implies prior deterioration of assets as a result of a period of continuing trading losses and/or cash outflows.

These financing constraints serve to reduce the variety of companies which are feasible acquisition prospects and effectively narrow the range over which it is worth searching for target companies. It is quite possible that the constraints imply that there are no feasible acquisitions which could meet the constraints. Alternatively there may be several target companies which satisfy the constraints and are consequently feasible acquisition prospects; in this case some means of ranking or choosing between them is required. In practice there are many further criteria which will influence target company selection such as product and factor markets positions, growth prospects, labour force considerations, existing shareholdings, type of acquisition – horizontal, vertical, conglomerate[6] etc; these aspects are not discussed further here other than by virtue of their financial implications. The selection process between feasible acquisitions is therefore regarded as a financial decision and, following the wealth maximizing viewpoint, may be specified in terms of selecting the acquisition which contributes most to the net present wealth of acquirer company shareholders. Preliminary interviews with experts indicated that top executives in F-type acquirer companies frequently held significant shareholdings in their companies; this suggests that shareholder net present wealth maximization was an appropriate overall acquisition objective.

Cash flows and distortions due to accruals accounting. The constraints implicitly related to investment as well as financing decisions since the overall objective of net present wealth maximization is measured by share price movements based upon expectations of dividend flows to investors. The latter are ultimately a result of cash flow generation from investment projects which, by current accuals accounting practice, are described as assets and earnings. Thus both the financing decision concerning the quantity and mix of investments and the investment decision concerning returns by way of earnings and assets per share are included in a combined model which allows overall optimization of shareholder net present wealth. An alternative cash flow perspective would substitute a constraint based upon dilution of cash flows per share instead of the dilution constraints on assets and earnings per share.

In fact the separation of earnings from assets is unfortunate in that differentia emphasis tends to be placed upon transactions in the profit and loss account as against transactions in the balance sheet although they are both no more nor less than approximations to cash flows. The financial press, as well as analysts and investors, tend to be concerned more with earnings than assets. Corporate taxes are based primarily upon earnings with special adjustments for asset cash flows such as investment incentives, contingent taxes on realized capital profits and depreciation allowances. Legal provisions relate to wasting assets, depreciation provisions, declaration of dividends 'out of capital' etc. Although the earlier discussion in Chapter 2 summarized the theoretical position that profit or 'earnings' should be regarded as a cash flow concept, there are relatively few investment analysts who concentrate primarily on cash flows per share as a means of assessing relative investment values. It may well be that a vicious circle exists connecting company information supplied to investors, information required by investors and information required by statute and by taxation authorities, thereby perpetuating the myth of accruals profit measures. To unravel whether such a vicious circle exists in reality would require further research into the information discounting processes of stock markets, to which reference was made in Chapter 2. Classification of information and of how various categories of investor employ information would be a useful contribution to research in this area.

Penalties if constraints are breached. Implicit in the concept of financial market imposed constraints is the idea of a 'loss function' relating to the consequences that arise if constraints are breached; this may be interpreted in terms of the risk of a fall in equity capitalization and is illustrated broadly in Figure 3:4. A fall in capitalization multiple could seriously affect the basis for future acquisitions in that the feasible region within short-term dilution constraints is thereby reduced.

The constraints of Figure 3:4 can be viewed as a process by which a company is progressively penalized for going further into the shaded area but that given a set of constraints there is a trade-off between being on the safe side of some and the unsafe side of others. The penalization would come about in terms of market capitalization of the financing instruments of the firm and would operate progressively upon equity and more secure instruments such as loans[7].

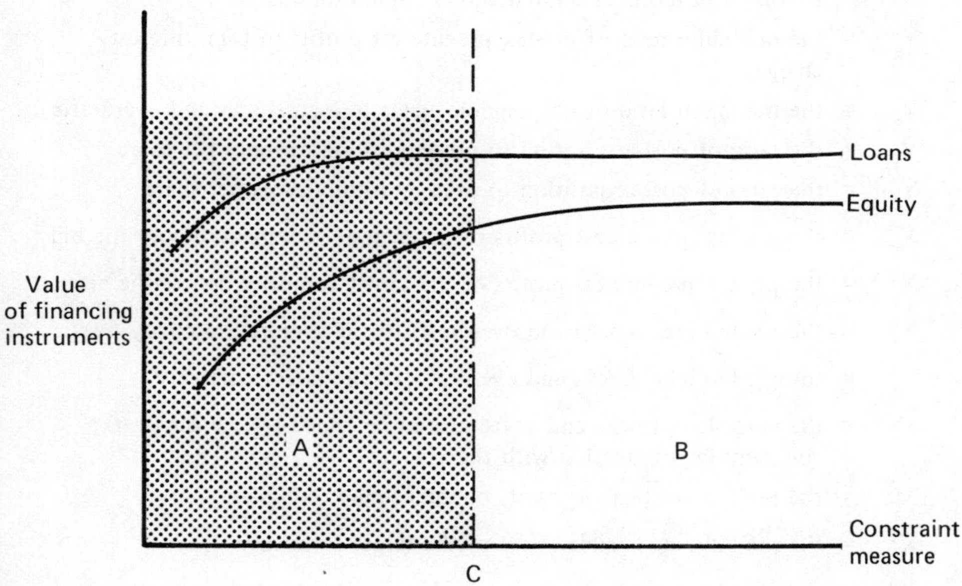

Area A: Area in which the constraint is violated - unsafe
Area B: Area in which the constraint is not violated - safe
Point C: Constraint level - an average concept linked to the type of company.

Figure 3:4 Effect of breaching a financial market constraint

Formalization of objectives and constraints in acquisition financing

In this section the financial constraints identified in the previous sections are given mathematical form under various assumptions. The variables relate to accruals accounting measures of earnings and assets but with the latter incorporating up-to-date revaluation of property in its current usage. The following notation is employed.

Let Y_i = the critical value for a particular constraint identified by the suffix i

X_j = the value of a variable identified by the suffix j which is an influence upon a constraint measure.

Thus the Y_i are the limiting levels of the constraints and the X_j are the values of the components such as assets, pre-tax earnings, equity capitalization, loans etc, which must fit into the constrained area. Specifically the Y_i and the X_j are defined by:

Y_1 = the maximum size of the acquisition relative to the acquirer's size measured in terms of quoted equity capitalizations

Y_2 = the minimum ratio of pre-tax pre-interest profits to total interest charges

Y_3 = the minimum ratio of net tangible assets to loan stocks and overdrafts

Y_4 = the ratio of post-acquisition to pre-acquisition earnings per share

Y_5 = the ratio of post-acquisition to pre-acquisition assets per share

X_1^A = the pre-tax pre-interest profits of the acquirer company before the bid

X_1^T = the pre-tax pre-interest profits of the target company before the bid

X_2^A = the pre-bid loan stocks and overdrafts of the acquirer company

X_2^T = the pre-bid loan stocks and overdrafts of the target company

δX_2^A = the extra loan stocks and overdrafts to be issued by the acquirer company in conjunction with the bid

X_3^A = the pre-bid net tangible assets of the acquirer company

X_3^T = the pre-bid net tangible assets of the target company

X_4^A = the pre-bid stock market value of the acquirer company's equity

X_4^T = the stock market value of the target company's equity

δX_4^A = the extra equity at expected stock market value to be issued by the acquirer company in conjunction with the bid

X_5^A = the pre-bid earnings available to ordinary shareholders of the acquirer after corporation tax and preference dividends

X_5^T = the pre-bid earnings available to ordinary shareholders of the target after corporation tax and preference dividends

X_6^A = the number of shares in issue of the acquirer prior to the bid

δX_6^A = the extra number of shares to be issued by the acquirer in conjunction with the bid

δX_7^A = the surplus cash of the acquirer company which is to be used in conjunction with financing the bid

I^A = the weighted average interest rate on the acquirer's loan stocks and overdrafts before the bid

I^T = the weighted average interest rate on the target's loan stocks and overdrafts before the bid

δI^A = the additional weighted average interest rate on the acquirer's loan stock and/or overdrafts which is to be issued in conjunction with the bid

S^A = the acquirer company's share price at the time of the bid.

Note: Net tangible assets are defined as net working capital less loans and preference capital plus net book valuations of tangible fixed assets adjusted for revaluation of land.

Financing objective. It was argued earlier that conceptually long-run net present wealth maximization for shareholders was the dominant objective for F-type companies. Given their opportunistic and entrepreneurial behaviour the practical translation of this objective into the problem of acquisition financing may be assumed to be consistent with minimizing the amount of equity capital issued in a particular acquisition, assuming the acquisition is to be made anyway. Evidently such a specification neglects long-term implications of particular financing mechanisms and in effect assumes that a solution within financial market constraints is a sufficient solution from the point of view of investors, ie it avoids any selling of shares on the ground of inappropriate financing (in the sense of unnecessarily risky, over-complex, unusual etc, which might cause investors to sell the company's shares on account of its altered financing). It also assumes that equity is the most expensive financing mechanism open to a firm in real world financial market conditions. Specifically the financing objective becomes:

> Minimize the equity content of the acquisition financing package, given the acquirer and target company financial states, subject to satisfaction of financial market constraints.

The variables in the financial package are δX_2^A, δX_4^A, δX_7^A, assuming that new issues of equity by the acquirer as part of the acquisition package are valued on a similar earnings multiple to that already in issue and that the interest rate requirements on the acquirer company's loan stocks are exogenous to the choice of financing method within feasible financing situations. It is assumed that extra cash in excess of δX_7^A is obtained by way of overdraft and is therefore incorporated into δX_2^A.

Relative size. This constraint is expressed in terms of relative equity capitalizations of the acquirer and target companies. Interview respondents indicated that unless a bid took the form of a reverse bid, generally a situation where the target company wants the acquirer's management in spite of being the larger company (and may therefore become the bidder), one would normally not try to bid for a larger company. Thus the hypothesized limit of Y_1 was taken as 1.0 and the constraint expression is given by (C1).

$$X_4^T \,/\, X_4^A \leqslant Y_1 \tag{C1}$$

Profits cover for interest charges. As a simplification, interest charges here refer to all loan stock and overdraft interest charges but do not include preference share interest since preference shares have a lower security than loans and overdrafts. The nature of the constraint is that all interest charges must be covered Y_2 times by pre-tax pre-interest profits. In the case of F-type companies, interview respondents noted a minimum value of $Y_2 = 2.0$ for times interest covered. This was a lower figure than merchant banks quoted for normal loan stocks but those interviewed suggested that the lower cover reflected a number of features specific to F-type company growth, in particular that since the loan stock related to acquisitions it was in effect sold to a captive market (target company shareholders) who were unlikely to quibble if the overall bid premium was attractive and a cash alternative was offered in the bid. In addition most bid loan stocks are convertibles and therefore have future equity rights which tend to lower interest coupons and may be a further reason for achieving lower covers. Y_2 was therefore hypothesized as 2.0 and the form of the constraint is given by (C2).

$$(X_1^A + X_1^T) \,/\, (I^A * X_2^A + I^T * X_2^T + \delta I^A * \delta X_2^A) \geqslant Y_2 \tag{C2}$$

Net tangibles cover for loan stocks. The same remarks apply to the cover limit on loan principle out of net tangible assets as for profits cover on interest charges; lower covers were quoted for F-type company acquisition loans than for normal loans issued for cash. Net tangibles covers were noted by those interviewed as being feasible down to approximately 1.0. Accordingly Y_3 was hypothesized to be 1.0. This means a one-to-one ratio could be reached of loans and preference shares to equity and reserves in acquisition financing. Specifically the constraint for net tangibles cover is given by (C3) below.

$$(X_3^A + X_3^T - \delta X_7^A) \,/\, (X_2^A + X_2^T + \delta X_2^A) \geqslant Y_3 \tag{C3}$$

Dilution in earnings per share of acquirer. Those interviewed were averse to financing acquisitions in which short-term dilution occurred in earnings per share. Whilst an acquisition could generally be 'pulled around' within a year to prevent any dilution being shown in earnings per share in the annual accounts, it was clearly preferable to avoid dilution possibilities. However in purchases of weak companies or loss-making situations, earnings per share dilution based upon past results is bound to arise and the question then really concerns the speed of turnround and rationalization which can be achieved post-acquisition. Together with the subsequent constraint of non-dilution in asset backing per share, one may expect circumstances in which earnings per share dilution may occur at the date of acquisition provided asset backing (and by implication potential future earnings) rises sharply. However as a hypothesis Y_4 was taken as 1.0 which implies a constraint of no dilution in earnings per share over the short term. Constraint (C4) formalizes this limit in the absence of preference shares forming part of the capital structure of either firm.

$$\frac{([(X_1^A + X_1^T) - (I^A*X_2^A + I^T*X_2^T + \delta I^A*\delta X_2^A)] \;/\; (X_6^A + \delta X_6^A))}{[(X_1^A - I^A*X_2^A) \;/\; X_6^A]} \geqslant Y_4 \qquad \text{(C4)}$$

Dilution in asset backing per share of acquirer. As for earnings per share, the response of those interviewed indicated an objective of avoiding dilution in asset backing per share. Indeed the overall consensus regarding objectives of growth for F-type companies placed great emphasis upon increasing shareholder wealth by asset backing and earnings per share growth together. Therefore it was hypothesized that the constraint $Y_5 = 1.0$, which amounts to no dilution in asset backing per share as a result of an acquisition.

$$\frac{[(X_3^A - \delta X_2^A - \delta X_7^A + X_3^T) \;/\; (X_6^A + \delta X_6^A)]}{[X_3^A \;/\; X_6^A]} \geqslant Y_5 \qquad \text{(C5)}$$

Acquisition value. There must be identify between the value of the acquisition instruments offered and the stock market capitalization of the target company's equity.

$$\delta X_2^A + \delta X_6^A * S^A + \delta X_7^A - X_4^T \equiv 0 \qquad \text{(C6)}$$

Number of shares issued. The number of shares issued at the acquirer company's share price must equal the value of acquirer company equity offered in the acquisition package.

$$\delta X_6^A * S^A - \delta X_4^A \equiv 0 \qquad \text{(C7)}$$

Objective function. The objective function for optimizing the bid financing decision was hypothesized to take the form, as already discussed, of minimizing the number of acquirer shares issued in the acquisition package. Formally this may be stated

$$\text{minimize } \delta X_6^A \text{ subject to constraints (C1) – (C7).}$$

Miscellaneous. Additional non-negativity constraints exist for both acquirer and target company variables:

$$X_2, \delta X_2, X_4, \delta X_4, X_6, \delta X_6, \delta X_7, I^A, I^T, \delta I^A, t, S^A \geqslant 0$$

The constraints $Y_1 - Y_5$ are assumed to remain constant over a period of time and relate to the circumstances of the combined acquirer and target company immediately after the bid. This assumes that ways are found round any intrusion upon S.54 of the 1948 Companies Act regarding the UK law against companies financing purchases of their own shares. In the absence of such a law δX_6^A could be < 0 but $|\delta X_6^A| < X_6^A$ although other practical constraints would probably apply. The values of the X_j 's are based upon most recent forecasts of the combining companies for the current year or the most recent accounts in the absence of forecasts. This information is normally contained in acquisition offer documents.

It is assumed that acquisitions are accounted for on a purchase basis and not on a pooling or merger basis. Further assumptions implicit in the above constraints are that the target company's capital structure is absorbed into that of the acquirer, that the earnings values X_1^A and X_1^T become the combined pre-tax pre-interest earnings in the short term for the combined companies and that constraints relate to the unconverted circumstances in cases where convertible loans with consequential deferred equity rights form part of the acquisition package.

An example of the calculation of constraint levels for an acquisition is given in Appendix 3.

Qualitative considerations – discussion

Interviews with experts in acquisition practice, although primarily concerned to clarify the impact of financial market constraints upon acquisition decisions, also yielded a considerable body of data on other acquisition considerations of a financial nature. These other considerations were largely qualitative and in some cases related only to particular acquirer company operations. However a number of factors appeared to be of general importance to the practice of acquisition and therefore worth reporting. The nature of the evidence was such that it does not reflect any sampling in a statistical sense but rather represents an assemblage of various interview comments which would require further research to substantiate adequately. Confidentiality aspects also prevent the author from reporting individual questionnaire responses and comments.

Assets and earnings distinctions. The theory of finance argument based upon a cash flow approach looks at asset values as a capitalization of future cash flows earned from the asset which, if discounted to equality with the asset cost, yield a rate of return on the asset. It has been argued earlier that F-type acquisitions which are successful for shareholders necessarily require incremental return or reduction of risk that cannot be achieved by shareholder portfolio adjustment but which require post-acquisition managerial action to alter flows of returns from the combined assets. Therefore the target company, which is selling assets to the acquirer presumably because either it lacks information about alternative higher yielding returns to the assets or the expertise to achieve such higher returns, values its assets lower than does the acquirer. Indeed a seller of an asset would not only need to have full information about a potential buyer's use of the asset in order to assess the value of the asset to the buyer but, to use that value as a bargaining counter in negotiating a sale price, the seller would also require the threat of being capable of redeploying the asset to that use by his own skills. Thus evaluation of assets in a balance sheet still only reflects the existing owner's values based upon cost and will only rarely be related closely to those of a potential purchaser. The seller's valuation would only be close to that of a potential purchaser if there was little scope for a changed earnings stream from the asset[8] or if the alternative earnings streams of the same asset in use by the acquirer and acquired firms were exactly compensated by differential discount rates. The latter is unlikely where the acquirer is increasing return or reducing risk as a general policy of growth. Revaluations of assets under conditions of imperfect information can only be an attempt to reach some revised idea of replacement cost conditioned on use of the assets within the owner firm.

The situation is also complicated in the case of publicly quoted companies by the link between investor expectations and value of a company's equity. Valuation of assets upwards within a firm to reflect a new use of them can only rationally be approved of, in the sense of increasing equity capitalization, by investors if they perceive that the managerial resources in the firm are adequate to secure an earnings stream accretion from those assets in excess of that derived from their existing use.

If it is agreed that the value of an asset reflects its future earnings stream but that there can be a wide variety of future earnings streams derivable from an asset depending upon managerial skills, risk, information about opportunities etc, then one can conceive of an asset as having a distribution of values reflecting the variety of its potential uses and users. To talk of asset backing for a share price is therefore a value judgment by the observer and depends on the observer's view of alternative uses and users of the assets of a firm; these uses may include a simple sale of the assets to a third party presumably at around the means of their value distributions less an amount to represent some notion of a 'normal return' which would vary with the product market conditions in which the asset is typically put to use.

In linking the foregoing discussion to F-type acquisition activity it is necessary to consider the asset structure of the target in the light of the acquirer company opportunities. The more target assets for which there are better earnings opportunities in the eyes of the acquirer then the more attractive the target becomes. This evidently depends considerably upon the skills that the former has in locating opportunities as well as in locating targets.

The interviews yielded data about the perceived practical, as opposed to conceptual distinctions between assets and earnings situations. Fixed assets which are not already secured provide a basis for further borrowing provided they are of a suitable quality, although borrowing also requires adequate profits to cover the servicing costs. Consequently assets can, through borrowing power, provide the means of investing in new earnings. The parts of a company which generate an earnings stream can be sold at a price based upon that earnings stream; this is the reverse of turning an asset into an earnings stream. The two processes together explain the idea noted by some acquirer company executives that one can 'reverse and see-saw' from assets to earnings. Release of assets from an operation also raises the 'efficiency of earnings' in relation to capital employed (ie the remaining net assets) and thereby augments the saleable value of the earnings. (The latter remark hides a collection of assumptions and experience about the way companies are valued in practice for sale purposes as earnings situations.) Experts tended to categorize acquisitions by F-type acquirers as 'assets situations' or 'earnings situations', the former being cases where the target was rich in assets but had a poor earnings record and the latter referring to a company with a good earnings growth record but low asset backing to its share price. The term 'asset-stripping', which in its purest form means that a target company is acquired with part or full equity consideration following which most of its assets are converted into cash before selling off the remnants, is essentially an alternative means of making a rights issue and has a useful role in raising cash in the early phase of an acquirer company's growth.

Of some interest is the idea that asset backing provides a risk-aversion element in an acquisition; several acquirers mentioned this point. This would appear to relate to the previous argument regarding alternative asset uses and bargaining power in bids. If the bidder has potential uses for the assets with rates of return well above the average that determines estimated 'market' prices for such assets he can indeed 'buy value at a discount' by purchasing the assets near the mean of the asset value distributions. On the other hand if an acquisition is bought primarily as an earnings situation then that target company is likely to be earning at least an average return on its assets in the sense of available alternative uses for them. Scope for creating added earnings from underutilized assets in earnings situations is naturally more limited and the means of combating 'risk' in existing earnings streams is correspondingly less. Several of the acquirers were deliberately not interested in acquiring earnings situations, and aimed to buy 'value at a discount' in terms of assets of target companies. Indeed the need to create earnings out of assets situation acquisitions is reinforced by the consequent earnings per share dilution implicit in bids where equity is given away or fixed interest commitments are incurred for no incremental earnings per share.

The main criteria which F-type acquirers sought in assets situations were investigated in the interviews. Especially important were land and buildings in the target which earned low returns and divisions of variable profitability where scope existed for cutting out loss-makers and expanding profitable activities. The existence of excess debtors, stocks and overhead costs were considered relevant to improving the efficiency of operating earnings of profitable target company divisions rather than in creating additional earnings from underused assets. Excess debtors, stocks and overheads were regarded as indicating the existence of bad management. None of the acquirers mentioned the use of comparative figures such as formal industry norms in making assessments of the level of stocks, debtors and overheads. However, acquirer company executives had ideas about achievable levels of profits on turnover and about the reductions they might be able to make in stocks and debtors, presumably based upon past experience.

The quality of assets was also stressed as being an important evaluation criterion; in particular asset backing was regarded as mainly based on property assets and did not take stocks into account. It was suggested that plant and machinery was not of great security value in depression periods due to its more limited realizability at such times.

In earnings situations it was difficult to make any generalizations about the target company selection criteria which F-type acquirers used, partly because few of the companies had ever bought a target company primarily for earnings purposes. However in relation to parts of assets situation targets, earnings situation criteria of return on assets can be relevant, eg in assessing the profitable parts of the target company; this was agreed by almost all the acquirers interviewed. Poor earnings performance of a company can also be an indication of assets situations. Miscellaneous comments noted included the need to assess future financing requirements of the target operating divisions and the stability or volatility of its earnings stream in view of the acquirer's objective of keeping a steadily growing earnings per share record.

Standing of acquirer company equity relative to market. The earnings multiple (P/E ratio) at which a company's equity is capitalized in financial markets is reported in the financial press as a measure of the share price relative to most recent historic earnings or available forecast of current annual earnings per share, based upon accrued measures of profit. Many of the experts attached considerable importance to maintaining a high capitalization multiple. The general view was that, early on in the life of an F-type acquirer company, the P/E ratio tends to be very high and stands at a considerable premium to net assets per share. For example two F-type acquirer companies which were studied as case studies had the following P/E ratios relative to the 500 All-Share

Index. The figures show that the relative level has tended to decline over the life of the acquirer company.

Company	Relative P/E ratios – 31 December			
	1970	1971	1972	1973
Acquirer A	∞	∞	2.85	0.72
Acquirer B	4.87	4.91	1.94	2.01

This premium was frequently referred to as the 'goodwill element' in the share price. To maintain such a goodwill element over a series of acquisitions requires that the high market rating 'rubs-off' on the valuation of each acquisition; some of those interviewed considered that this was more likely to happen if the acquisitions comprised purchases of several relatively small companies rather than a few relatively large target companies. In addition or possibly as a cause of perceived failure for a high P/E rating to rub-off on 'too large' an acquisition, is the consideration of risk arising as a result of an acquisition. Several smaller acquisitions would provide a more stable earnings portfolio based on existing or future earnings streams (unless the streams were perfectly correlated). The acceptability of acquisition consideration such as loan stocks and equity to the seller shareholders is another factor which can limit acquisition size; however this point is dealt with subsequently in discussion of offer packages and institutional investors' valuation of acquirer paper.

These ideas could be interpreted as a confusion between the approximation of accrued assets and earnings measures to actual cash flows. Companies growing by acquisition and rationalization of acquired assets will tend to have considerable balance sheet cash flows as a result of capital changes and asset realizations whereas the profit and loss account cash flows are often of lesser magnitude. Consequently until the latter outweigh the former a valuation measure based upon either historic actual or current year forecasts of accrued earnings is bound to be extremely high if investors are rationally focussing upon cash flow measures. Given expectations of growth in cash flows then a premium on asset valuation is also likely. Prescriptively one might suggest the it is better to focus upon cash flow growth of assets and/or earnings rather than worry about maintaining a P/E multiple.

Minimum size of acquisitions. Those interviewed were asked whether they considered that there was a minimum size of target for which acquirers would consider bidding. Respondents were unable to attach measures to this minimum but all the five acquirer respondents to the question agreed that there was a minimum relative size of acquisition in cases where the acquisition objective was not simply to round out an operating unit. This minimum size was conceived of as adequate to make some clear impact upon acquirer assets and/or earnings and as sizeable enough to justify managerial input to the acquisition.

Influence of stock market conditions. Most of the experts considered that the state of the stock market affected acquisition activity. In particular the attitude of investors to the loan stock component of acquisition financing packages varied; in bullish markets convertible loan stock tended to be viewed as deferred equity whereas in bearish markets it tended to be viewed as straight loan stock. Institutional investors were reluctant to accept straight loan stock as acquisition consideration without any equity rights, especially in bull markets; cash consideration was regarded as attractive in bear market conditions. The danger to acquirer market rating of having equity on sale as a result of a bid involving paper provides a further argument for acquirers to prefer cash offer packages during bearish markets. Coupon rates on convertibles were thought to reflect interest rates at the time of issue together with a reduction depending upon the extent of conversion rights into equity. The volatility of the company's earnings stream would exhibit itself in the loan stock interest coupon, higher variability implying higher risk to lenders and therefore a premium on the required interest rate. The issue of convertible loan stock imposes contingent implications for cash flows and equity capital adjustment in that conversion dilutes the equity base. The issue of warrants to subscribe also dilutes issued equity if the warrants are taken up but also contributes an inflow of cash at the same time. Clearly the probability of subscription or conversion depends upon stock market conditions. Institutional investors were also averse to complex bids with instruments which made packages hard to evaluate, particularly where convertibles or other forms of future equity rights existed; warrants were not approved of. The institutional investors who were interviewed were quite prepared to sell shares in the market when they disagreed with a bid.

Evidence of activity in acquisitions was noted by several of those interviewed as a positive factor in improving the market rating of acquirers in bull market conditions.

Commercial logic. The majority of those interviewed mentioned the need for 'commercial logic' in acquisition deals. This need was seen as requiring that an acquisition should link up with existing product and/or factor market commitments of the acquirer company. The closest description of the idea was that an F-type acquirer should develop a small number of specialist activities which subsequent acquisitions should complement. Pure conglomerate acquisitions were frowned upon although if an acquirer company had proved its success in rationalizing target companies with consequent increments to assets and earnings per share it was felt that investors would place less emphasis on the need for commercial logic. The idea of a requisite minimal commercial logic, which decreases with a good track record by acquirer management, may be interpreted as defining expected earnings stream volatility after an acquisition, in terms of expected managerial input needs from the acquirer to the target company, modified by the acquirer track record in dealing with such situations, and coupled with some notion of covariance in the combined prospective earnings streams. The expected managerial input would increase as the industrial separation of the acquirer and target companies increased with the relative size of the acquisition but would decrease with the extent of readily realizable assets in the target. The latter point hypothesizes that it is only the earnings parts of asset-situation acquisitions which require extensive industrial managerial inputs. Realization of assets is a shorter time scale managerial input by the acquirer to the target and relates to the quality of the acquisition deal rather than to longer term rationalization of the target company's production and marketing activities.

Legal and fiscal matters. Readers interested in the detailed legal and taxation considerations involved in acquisitions should consult the comprehensive book by Weinberg (1971) concerning UK provisions and practices.

The legal influence on offer packages largely revolves around section 54 of the 1948 Companies Act which is designed primarily to prevent a company buying its own shares. Target companies rich in assets and with little debt structure can in theory be acquired merely with a bridging loan which is repaid out of asset realizations in the target after the acqusition. Although the legal rulings are not completely clear it would appear that the bridging loan scheme would fall foul of section 54 unless the bidder is capable of raising the acquisition consideration on the basis of its own balance sheet without recourse to target company assets. Section 54 also affects the use of secured debentures as acquisition instruments since they cannot be secured on the target company assets in the same way as unsecured loan stocks effectively are where insufficient net tangibles cover exists in the acquirer alone to raise the acquisition loan stocks.

There are many fiscal factors to consider in any particular acquisition such as carry-forward and set-off of losses, depreciation allowance benefits, extent of control and group tax status etc. Although tax planning is an important aspect of acquisition planning it is a highly specialized subject and outside the scope of this book. However it is worth mentioning one important tax factor in most acquisitions, namely the liability of seller shareholders, whether corporate or individual, to capital gains tax upon realized gains on share disposals. The effect of this is that shareholders who receive an all-cash or part-cash/part-paper bid for shares which they hold in a company fall liable to gains tax on any gain apportioned to the cash part of the consideration, and have a contingent liability to gains tax on any gain apportioned to the paper part of the consideration; the latter is taxable when the paper is disposed of. Thus although cash is the most certain consideration which a seller shareholder can receive it also suffers an immediate tax liability. A further tax factor which affects some institutional investors is that their tax system allows them to set off dividends received against dividends paid and therefore an acquisition which substitutes loan stock interest (unfranked investment income) for dividends (franked investment income) can be somewhat unattractive if the institution has no loan stock gearing.

Accounting for acquisitions. The accounting aspects investigated were first whether merger or acquisition accounting methods were used, second how goodwill arising on acquisition was dealt with, and third how pre-acquisition profits and losses are taken into published accounts. In addition to results of interviews, Extel cards were reviewed for a number of F-type acquirers; the review suggested that the accounting practices of the interview respondents were not unusual.

The purchase accounting procedure was used in all cases, based upon Extel reviews and supported by the case histories discussed subsequently. Goodwill which arose as a result of acquisition tended to be written off against reserves; the desire to avoid creating goodwill, which is not generally available as security for borrowings, is a further incentive to keep acquisition purchase prices in line with revaluations of acquired assets and vice versa. Consequently acquirer companies tend to write-up acquired assets as much as possible to minimize if not avoid goodwill creation and in some cases write-off surplus goodwill against reserves.

Interview respondents considered that investors were prepared to accept exceptional losses from acquisitions in the year of purchase. This facilitates excessive first-year loss writedown with a view to creating a cushion for future profits: for example an excessive stock writedown in the year of acquisition could help to boost accounting profits for subsequent periods.

Respondents did not have rigid methods of accounting for pre- and post-acquisition profits and the impression gained was that practices in this accounting area could be quite flexible.

Reported earnings per share can be adjusted downwards if necessary by making an acquisition before the end of the year, as a result of which the overall equity base of the acquirer company increases. Reported profits remain the same provided the acquired firm's earnings are taken into pre-acquisition profits which are capitalized. This practice allows some cushioning for future reported earnings.

Evidence from case studies

Information concerning the level of the constraints was derived from the interviews with experts in acquisition practice and also from detailed case studies of acquisitions. The results of the interviews have been incorporated into the constraint values noted in the section 'Funding Constraints' earlier in this chapter; the values were:

Maximum size	Y_1	=	1.0
Times interest cover	Y_2	=	2.0
Net tangibles cover	Y_3	=	1.0
Relative earnings/share	Y_4	=	1.0
Relative assets/share	Y_5	=	1.0

Two active F-type acquirer companies were chosen as suitable subjects for case studies. The objective of the case studies was to provide detailed information about F-type acquisition activity of a qualitative and a quantitative nature. Selection of the two case study companies was achieved by reference to one of the experts, namely a financial journalist who was familiar with F-type acquisitions. He was asked to select two active and successful acquirer companies. The case study analysis acted as a check of the interview results.

Constraint levels calculated. Data for the case studies came entirely from publicly issued documents such as annual reports, offer documents, press cuttings and investment press comments. Two F-type acquirer companies, labelled Acquirer A and Acquirer B, were studied in depth over the period up to August 1972 from the start of their acquisition activity. During that time Acquirer A bought three publicly quoted companies and Acquirer B bought five public companies. For each acquisition the constraint levels of the final acquisition terms were calculated; if the constraints were beyond the limits noted above they were regarded as critical and if they were within the limits they were regarded as non-critical. Figure 3:5 summarizes the critical and non-critical constraints for each acquisition.

If the form of the constraints and objective function outlined in the previous section is considered from a programming viewpoint then if the acquirer is optimizing the financing package it would be expected that at least one constraint in each deal is at a critical level but not significantly below that level.

The results indicate:

1 All acquisitions have at least one constraint which is critical when compared to the hypothesized values of the Y_i 's.

2 Three of the eight acquisitions have two critical constraints but none has more than two critical constraints (out of a possible but unlikely five critical constraints).

3 Only three of the 11 critical constraints for all acquisitions lie more than 10% from the hypothesized critical levels. They are:

Acquirer A, Target A-1	Y_1
Acquirer A, Target A-3	Y_4
Acquirer B, Target B-1	Y_4

In the two cases where constraint Y_4 was violated by more than 10% (Target A-3 and Target B-1) both target companies were making substantial losses and had little hope of recovery into a profitable situation except by drastic rationalization. In both cases the acquirer company's asset backing rose sharply as a result of the bid. Overall therefore the results would seem to support the hypothesized constraint levels and the model form.

Deal quality. The constraints and the objectives of maximizing net present shareholder wealth, ie the level of a company's share price, imply that the quality of a deal is related to the added assets and earnings per share consequent upon an acquisition. Specifically, a well-conceived deal will add to both assets and earnings per share and thus provide an incentive for investors to bid up the company's share price.

A measure of the association between share price changes and changes in assets and earnings per share can be seen from Figure 3:7 and 3:8. In these the immediate increases/decreases in earnings and assets per share as a result of the acquisition deal are shown alongside share price changes. Following the results of interviews which suggested that there was some trade-off between increments in assets per share and dilution in earnings per share or vice versa, the tabulated signs of changes relate to cases where constraints have been breached to the extent of more than 10%. Thus if immediate earnings per share as a result of an acquisition had not been diluted by more than 10% the sign was positive but if the dilution was more than 10% the sign given was negative. Similar procedures were used for assets per share dilution signs.

The results show that share price movements tend to move in the direction expected as a result of changes in assets and earnings per share with a slight bias towards association with assets per share changes. This would be consistent with the idea that the market discounts future earnings increments consequent upon post-acquisition managerial action which is expected to yield additional earnings from underutilized assets.

Indication of returns from acquisitions by F-type case study companies. Published financial data does not allow the evaluation of ex-post discounted cash flow rates of return from investment projects; however some idea of the returns from the acquisitions of Figure 3:5 made by the F-type case study acquirer companies A and B can be gleaned from the data shown in Figure 3:6. This indicates the approximate undiscounted payback period for each of the acquisitions of Figure 3:5 together with an assessment of the longer-term benefits for which quantitative measures are not readily made. The main points to note are the very fast payback of the acquisitions and the fact that after a fast payback there were useful longer-term benefits to reap either from property development or from rationalized operations.

Acquirer company	Target company	Constraints					Number critical
		Relative size (Y_1)	Loan stock interest cover (Y_2)	Loan stock assets cover (Y_3)	Dilution in earnings/share (Y_4)	Dilution in assets/share (Y_5)	
Acquirer A	Target A-1	C (1.2)	NC	NC	NC	C (0.9)	2
	Target A-2	NC	C (1.9)	NC	NC	NC	1
	Target A-3	NC	NC	NC	C (0.7)	NC	1
Acquirer B	Target B-1	NC	C (1.8)	NC	C (0.6)	NC	2
	Target B-2	C (1.1)	NC	NC	NC	NC	1
	Target B-3	NC	C (1.9)	NC	NC	NC	1
	Target B-3	NC	C (1.9)	NC	C (0.9)	NC	2
	Target B-4	NC	NC	NC	NC	C (0.9)	1

Notes: C Constraint in question is critical, ie beyond the relevant limit of Y .

NC Constraint in question is non-critical, ie within the relevant limit of Y .

The limits used for the critical values of the constraints were:

$$Y_1 = 1.0,\ Y_2 = 2.0,\ Y_3 = 1.0,\ Y_4 = 1.0,\ Y_5 = 1.0$$

Dilution here means the ratio of post:pre-acquisition measures.

Figure 3:5 Post-acquisition actual constraint values

Acquirer	Target company	Payback period (A)	Longer-term benefits (D)	
			Property (B)	Operations (C)
A	A–1	164% in 1 year	negligible	negligible
	A–2	approx. 1 year	freehold site retained	moderate
	A–3	within 2 years	small	very substantial
B	B–1	164% in 2 years	none	none
	B–2	113% in 2 years	substantial development	none
	B–3	more than 2 years	substantial development	substantial
	B–4	85% in 1 year	very substantial	moderate
	B–5	185% in 1 year	substantial development	moderate

Notes: (A) Conservative estimates:
The figures for payback do not reflect the time value of money. A more sophisticated approach would introduce such considerations by discounting or charging opportunity interest costs. However the objective of the table would not be greatly aided by this extra refinement.

(B) Benefits by way of future property developments.

(C) Benefits by way of retained operating companies.

(D) Benefits after two years from acquisition date.

Figure 3:6 Summary of returns from acquisitions by the case study companies A, B

Acquirer company	Target company	Assets/ share	Earnings/ share	Increase (+)/ Decrease (–) in acquirer's share price (A)	
				Shorter-term (B)	Longer-term (C)
Acquirer A	Target A–1	+	+	+	+
	Target A–2	+	+	+	+
	Target A–3	+	–	–	–
Acquirer B	Target B–1	+	–	+	+
	Target B–2	+	+	+	+
	Target B–3	+	+	+	+
	Target B–4	+	+	+	+
	Target B–5	+	+	–	+

Notes: (A) Share price movements are calculated as the share movement relative to the FT Actuaries All-Share Index.

(B) Movement of the share price up (+) or down (–) two months after bid from the price at the date of the bid.

(C) Movement of the share price up (+) or down (–) at the date of the next bid, or by June 1972 if earlier, from the price at the date of the bid.

Figure 3:7 Changes in assets and earnings per share, changes in longer- and shorter-term share prices consequent upon acquisitions

Share price* changes	Direction	Assets/ share	Earnings/ share
Shorter- term	same	6	6
	different	2	2
Longer- term	same	7	6
	different	1	2

* See Figure 3:7 for distinction of 'longer' and 'shorter' terms.

Note: A sign test based upon the differences in directions between share price assessments and movements in assets and earnings per share shows that the direction of longer-term movements in share prices and changes in assets per share were significantly associated (95% confidence limit). Associations in direction of change between the other elements of the table were all within 85% confidence limits. Although a 95% confidence limit is the usual criterion for associative tests, given the low number of data points the other associations should not be dismissed.

Figure 3:8 Share price changes compared with assets and earnings per share changes for case study acquirer companies consequent upon an acquisition

Share incentive schemes and directors' shareholdings. Most F-type acquirer companies provide share incentive schemes for key executives; both case study companies created schemes for their executives. These schemes had an upper limit to the number of shares which could be issued and the main aspects of each are outlined below.

Acquirer A

Restricted shares are entitled to only a percentage of ordinary dividends but rank in full for scrip or rights issues. Quotation of issues of restricted shares is geared to earnings per share on ordinary shares whereupon they rank *pari passu* with ordinary shares.

Acquirer B

Ordinary shares are available for issue partly paid to executives. Partly paid shares do not confer rights to dividends and have restricted voting rights.

Figure 3:9 shows the directors' shareholdings in aggregate for each of the case study companies. The shareholdings include shares issued under incentive schemes but mainly reflect the shareholdings arising from the original takeover of the companies by directors and their associates.

	Acquirer A	Acquirer B
% of ordinary issued capital	19.3	6.9
Market value of shareholdings (1)	£0.49m	£1.59m
Number of directors – total (2)	5	6
Annual remuneration – total (2)	£32 200	£43 500

Source: Extel cards

Notes: (1) For the company year of account ended in 1971.
(2) Figures relate to the accounting year of the company which covers the major part of 1971.

Figure 3:9 Directors' shareholdings in case study companies

It is evident that the personal financial positions of directors are much more sensitive to movements in their companies' share prices than to emoluments received; furthermore the provisions of the share incentive schemes are geared to capital gains rather than dividend income. To this extent there are clear financial motivations for directors to pursue rational financial policies in conducting their company's affairs. If it can be assumed that share prices are primarily based upon future income streams to shareholders then the evidence supports net present shareholder wealth maximization as an appropriate description of conceptual objectives of directors in these companies.

Frequency of deals. A deal is defined here as an acquisition or disposal of a company or assets of sufficient materiality to be reported in the press or in financial results of the dealing company. The 1967 Companies Act requires firms to disclose in their directors' reports significant changes in the principal activities and in fixed assets during the accounting period. In addition Stock Exchange regulations regarding quoted companies require companies to publish data regarding any material acquisitions or disposals of assets or subsidiaries.

The activity of the case study companies in terms of acquisition dealing can be assessed by the number of deals made from the date at which the current executive team took control until August 1972, the closing date of this case study analysis.

Acquirer A made eighteen deals during the period from August 1970; Acquirer B made fifteen deals during the period from October 1969. Neither of these companies reported substantial investment projects of an internal nature not directly consequent upon an acquisition. Acquirer A acquired three public companies and Acquirer B acquired five public companies, all within the period January 1970 to April 1972 inclusive.

A perspective on the relative activity of these two companies to the group of companies classified in Appendix 2 as being financially-oriented can be obtained from Figure 3:10. This shows the distribution of publicly quoted company acquisitions made by the 'F-type' group over the period 1 January 1970 to 30 April 1972.

The average number of acquisitions of UK publicly quoted companies made by an F-type acquirer over the period was 2.9; thus the two case study companies were relatively active in making acquisitions of publicly quoted companies.

Number of acquisitions made in the period	1	2	3	4	5	6	7	8+
Number of F-type acquirers which made the above number of acquisitions in the period	8	10	9	3	2	1	1	1

Figure 3:10 Acquisitions of UK publicly quoted companies by F-type acquirers during the period 1 January 1970 to 30 April 1972

Summary

The discussion in this chapter has argued that financially-oriented acquisition activity should be seen as an adaptive phenomenon which is restricted by financial market constraints. These constraints operate simultaneously on the financing decision by way of covers on debt interest and capital and on the investment decision by way of incremental returns to shareholders based upon expectations of accretion to assets and earnings per share.

Acquisition activity in general is associated with stock market price movements. Bids offering cash alternatives are more frequent in relation to total bids during conditions of falling as opposed to rising stock markets.

Returns resulting from acquisition activity tend to be analysed in terms of assets and earnings per share rather than cash flows. Particular emphasis in financially-oriented acquisition activity concerns the purchase and rationalization of asset-rich target companies, especially those with substantial property assets. The case study companies achieved high returns from their acquisitions.

Capitalization multiples are a measure of short-term earnings only; consequently if asset backing per share rises rapidly as a result of acquisition policy the P/E ratio is bound to be high. The concept of a 'goodwill element' in share prices during the early phase of acquisition growth by a financially-oriented acquirer company reflects expectations of asset- and earnings-derived cash flows and may be interpreted as an overall expectation of increments to net cash flow per share.

Case histories of two successful financially-oriented acquirer companies show that, following acquisition announcements, the direction of change in their share price ratio to the FT Index corresponds to changes in assets and earnings per share. The case histories also support the model of acquisition activity constrained by financial market funding limitations.

The key executives in financially-oriented acquirer companies tend to have equity shareholdings in their companies. For the two case studies these shareholdings were relatively more important than annual emoluments; rationally therefore such executives would be motivated towards shareholder wealth maximizing behaviour.

Financially-oriented acquirer companies are more active in acquisition activity than other companies.

Notes

1 The divergence between the interests of managers and shareholders features widely in behavioural theories of the firm such as those of Cyert and March (1963). Williamson (1967) has made an extension study of managerial discretionary behaviour.

2 See for example studies using discriminant analysis such as Kuehn (1968), Altman (1968).

3 The author's unpublished PhD thesis contains details of the research process. See D.G. Bean, 'Financial Strategy in Acquisition Decisions', unpublished PhD thesis, Manchester Business School, 1973.

4 See Cyert and March (1963), Simon (1955) (1964).

5 For example refer to the paper by R.L. Nelson in Alberts and Segall (1966).

6 Ansoff (1968) suggests detailed procedures for external investment and develops classifications for types of acquisition.

7 Figure 3:4, which is consistent with the traditional view of financial markets, is not totally at odds with the Modigliani and Miller studies due to their later revisions – refer to Modigliani and Miller (1958), (1963), (1966). Readers wishing to follow up the idea that loans progressively take up some of the penalties of moving into the unsafe area might find interest in a study of the Penn-Central debacle in Gordon (1971). The idea of financial market constraints follow those of Marris (1966).

8 Marris (1966), p. 33, also discusses differential valuation of assets from a similar viewpoint.

4 Strategy for Bidding and Financing

Introduction

In any trading operation cost minimization is as important a goal as maximization of returns; acquisition activity is no exception. Reduction in acquisition size for a given set of target assets and earnings will increase the incremental assets and earnings per share of the acquirer by way of reduced financing costs. Relative strength in acquisition bargaining may be expected to influence total size, ie equity capitalization, of the target company at its acquisition exit valuation. Stapleton (1971) has presented a theoretical analysis of bargaining between the combining companies in an acquisition; also the interviews and case studies concerning F-type acquirers suggest a model of acquisition-bargaining strategy aimed at reducing overall acquisition cost. These pieces of theoretical and empirical analysis are integrated into a discussion of bargaining objectives for reduction of acquisition cost.

The second area where acquisition cost can be reduced arises in the selection of suitable financing instruments. Although the debt content is bounded overall by way of net tangibles and interest cover constraints, these leave some latitude for choice in the selection of convertible loan stocks and deferred equity rights as a means of reducing short-term interest charges – albeit at some long-term cost to shareholders in contingent equity dilution. Baumol, Malkiel and Quandt (1966) have presented a theoretical model for valuation of convertible loan stocks, and studies by Merton (1973) and by Black and Scholes (1973) make the link between the nature of stock market prices and the pricing of corporate financing instruments. Models are discussed with a view to making prescriptive suggestions for selection of suitable acquisition instruments which minimize financing costs to acquirer company shareholders.

Negotiation issues

The previous chapter argued that a bid is only likely to be worthwhile to investors if the acquirer company is able to put the acquired company's assets to use in higher-return and/or lower-risk activities as a result of managerial inputs which could not be achieved equally well by portfolio adjustment of investors. The change in value of the target company's assets as a result of changed ownership represents a gain which has to be distributed in some proportion between the old and new owners of the assets, who are respectively the target and acquirer company shareholders. Acquisition bargaining therefore concerns negotiation of the proportions attributable to each shareholder group.

Bid premiums

It is usually assumed that a bid must be at a premium over the existing price level of the target company's shares so that target company shareholders are given an incentive to accept the offer. Newbould (1970) found that bid premiums averaged around a third above the pre-bid share price for acquisitions in general. However the notion that a bid premium is a necessity assumes that expectations of a bid imply a share price lower than the ultimate bid level and that the quoted share price is a good indication of valuation of the target company. It is suggested that these two factors are interrelated together with the distribution of shareholdings in the target company. The issues may be clarified by using the simple model outlined below.

$$V = E(V) \equiv p\,V_B + (1 - p)\,V_A \tag{1}$$

where V is the value of a company's shares in the market and equals the expected value $E(V)$
V_B is the value of the company's shares given a bid
V_A is the value of the company's shares given no bid
V_Q is the value per target company share to the acquirer
p is the probability of a bid.

From (1) and the fact that $0 \leqslant p \leqslant 1$

$$0 \leqslant p \equiv \frac{(V/V_A) - 1}{(V_B/V_A) - 1} \leqslant 1 \tag{2}$$

and therefore if

$$V_B \geqslant V_A \quad \text{then} \quad V_A \leqslant V \leqslant V_B \tag{3}$$

or if

$$V_B \leqslant V_A \quad \text{then} \quad V_B \leqslant V \leqslant V_A \tag{4}$$

Generally situation (3) occurs and therefore the market value of a company's shares stands at a premium over V_A depending upon the possibility of a bid. Situation (4) however is not without interest. In efficient stock markets the quoted share price of a company is the price at which marginal sellers trade with marginal buyers and does not reflect 'intrinsic worth' except in so far as marginal sellers' and buyers' expectations of price changes are based upon such concepts[1]. Where the shareholdings of a company are widely distributed so that no shareholder holds a block of shares which cannot be sold close to the market price then each shareholder will have expectations of value at or above V_A because if a bid is made below V_A there is no reason to accept; similarly $p = 0$ at V_A since potential bidders cannot expect acceptance of bids below V_A. The situation is illustrated by case 1 of Figure 4:1. If however one shareholder holds a block of shares of such a size that he cannot sell them without depressing the market price, he can only expect to realize an average price for his share of $\bar{V}$ which is less than V. Consequently a bid for shares at above $\bar{V}$ will have attractions for him even though it may be unattractive to other shareholders who could hope to sell near the marginal market price V. Case 2 of Figure 4:1 illustrates this situation and corresponds to situation (4) above.

Consequently the acquirer company can expect to achieve a lower bid price relative to the current market price where the target company has a high concentration of shareholdings in a few hands. It is also interesting to note how leakage of bid information would affect share prices in the two cases. Leakage of information would produce marginal transactions at V nearer V_B since the probability of a bid in the eyes of transacting investors would be higher. Consequently in case 1 the market price of the target company's shares would tend to rise whereas in case 2 the price would tend to fall.

The discussion has only considered the situation of a single bidding company. However it is likely that case 2 type companies will have more potential bidders than case 1 type companies given the same basis of capitalization of returns. This arises directly from Figure 4:1. A rational acquirer company which values a target company at V_Q would need to have V_Q above V to consider bidding for case 1 type companies whereas V_Q need only be above $\bar{V}$ to facilitate a feasible bid for case 2 types companies. As a result it will be especially in the latter's interest to attempt to obtain a contested bid if a takeover appears likely. Newbould (1970) has pointed out that once a contested-bid situation occurs the bid premiums that are realized tend to be substantially larger than in uncontested situations. Conversely from the acquirer's viewpoint if a bid can be agreed with dominant shareholders of a case 2 type company prior to a public offer then the scope for achieving exceptional returns from the acqusition is substantially enhanced.

Bargaining models

A model of merger bargaining and financing strategy has been developed by Stapleton (1971) following an earlier game-theoretic approach to business combinations by Mossin (1968). Stapleton considers the case of two combining companies A and B, which will be interpreted in the context of F-type acquisition activity as the (larger) acquirer and the (smaller) target companies respectively. It is assumed that prior to negotiations each company has knowledge of the other's alternative courses of action to the combination and that the combination can result in the best opportunities for both companies. Two possible ways of distributing the overall gains from the combination to the sets of shareholders in A and B are considered by Stapleton, namely equal percentage gain and equal absolute gain. The former distributes the gain in proportion to the capitalizations of A and B and the latter distributes half of the gain to each body of shareholders.

Gain distribution in the Stapleton model. Under conditions where the gains to the acquisition are uncertain and the acquisition consideration is entirely equity Stapleton shows that each company should exaggerate the profitability of its alternative courses of action and also seek to influence the other's view of the benefits of the deal. Specifically A, the acquirer company, should seek to minimize the expectations of B, the target company, regarding the acquisition gains, whereas B should seek to influence A's expectations upwards. When possibilities of debt or cash-financing considerations are introduced further implications derive from the model, as follows:

1. If B's expectations of overall acquisition benefit are less than those of A then A can benefit by offering cash or debt.
2. If B's expectations exceed those of A then A would do better to offer equity – however in practice the tax advantages of debt may be dominant.
3. Differing expectations are primarily relevant where the equal gain solution is likely. Under equal percentage gain and full equity considerations differing expectations are irrelevant.
4. Bargaining strategy implicitly precedes financing strategy – although in practice the two processes may operate iteratively until both a suitable valuation and a suitable financing package are arrived at for the target company.

Point 1 above is consistent with the results noted in the previous chapter which showed that cash consideration was more favoured during falling stock markets.

Stapleton also argued that if the marginal utilities of wealth for the two sets of shareholders in A and B are equal then the equal-gain solution is the more logical since one set of shareholders would lose more relative to the other if the combination did not in fact proceed to completion. The increasingly accepted view that managers of companies who are divorced from ownership tend to benefit from growth in sales and staff rather than profitability[2] has implications for the bargaining position that they may adopt where a bid is agreed by them on behalf of shareholders rather than directly by shareholders. Personal job security and fringe benefits may be jeopardized by target company directors who pursue the more ambitious target of equal gain as opposed to equal percentage gain. The financial press frequently analyses offers on the basis of percentages of assets and earnings contributed as compared with percentage of combined equity obtained. Consequently there are several reasons why the target company, presumed to be the smaller of the combining parties, will tend to accept acquisition terms lower than the equal-gain solution especially if bid terms are negotiated and agreed by target company directors rather than shareholders. The converse would tend to be true if the acquirer has a management largely divorced from ownership whereas the target company directors have significant shareholdings; in such a case the former may be prepared to accept even less than an equal-gain solution to extend the sales and staff under their control whereas the latter will aim to maximize the gain to shareholders of the target company.

Results of interviews with experts. The experts were asked to indicate their expectations of minimum offer premiums required in a bid to render the bid attractive to seller shareholders. All but one considered that there were no uniform guidelines on offer premiums although asset backing was an influence where it was not already discounted in the pre-bid share price. Indeed high-asset backing was regarded as a useful basis for defending against unwanted bids.

A number of points relating to bid strategy arose from answers to this question, in particular that shareholdings in the target acquired prior to the bid can serve as a means of keeping the premium down. Where there is the possibility of a third-party bid the acquirer is faced with the choice of making a first bid as a pre-emptive strategy or of making a 'sighting shot' which could result in a counter-offer (and, in the experience of two acquirers, requiring the exercise of some personal restraint to avoid bidding 'too high just to win the battle'). However the existence of a third-party bid can at least create a dealing profit which removes some of the risk of bidding in potentially contested situations.

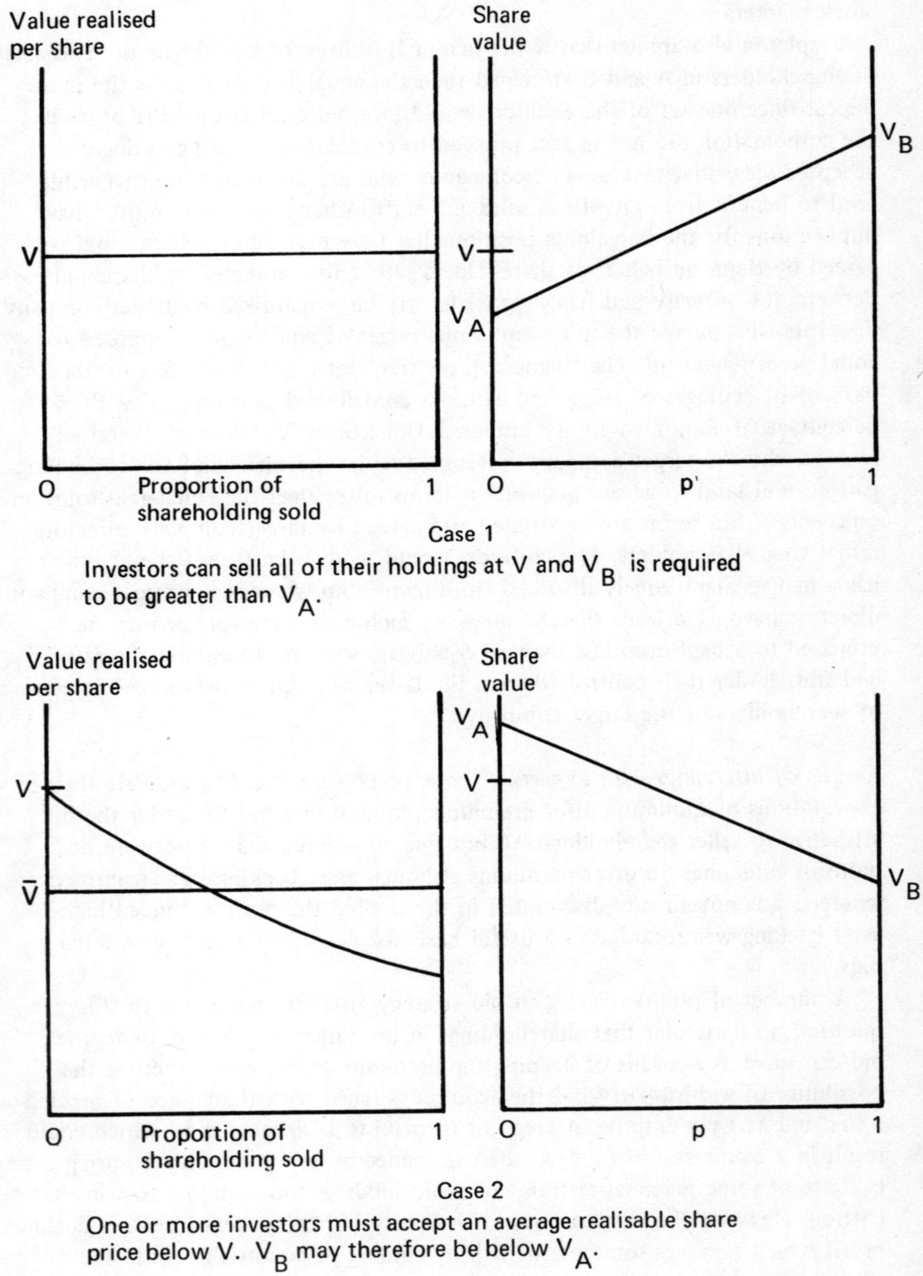

Figure 4:1 Realizable values per share in target companies

The importance of obtaining as much target company equity as possible in advance of the bid[3] either in terms of verbal support or by more formal means such as irrevocable acceptances prior to the bid was stressed by all the respondents. This was regarded as especially important where large blocks of shareholders existed in the target company. However even if there is considerable support for a bid arranged in advance some premium is generally considered necessary over the pre-bid price. An additional factor in gauging the likely reception of the bid amongst target shareholders and the necessary premium level is the past performance of the target. The further point that in an agreed bid there can be relatively tight cover constraints on loan stocks in the acquisition package makes it even more worthwhile for acquirers to try to agree bids in advance. The process of creating an offer package and its acceptance by the target company shareholders appeared to represent a feasible solution arranged between two bargaining parties and their advisers, normally merchant bankers, one of whose main functions is to arrange a suitable offer package within financial market constraints. The two parties can have varying degrees of bargaining power depending upon their equity stakes in the target; evidently the greater the bargaining power of the acquirer the greater is his opportunity of achieving maximal returns from the acquisition joint financing and investment decision. Market operations, which are discussed next, provide the acquirer with additional negotiating power. The term market operations refers here to various practices which are performed in the stock market to provide more effective control over bargaining power in bids and to cause deliberate impact upon share prices.

Market operations

This section only discusses some of the more widely practised operations noted by interviewees. Alterations have been made to the City Code and company law reforms have been proposed since this study was completed. The advantages of building up pre-bid equity stakes in a firm have been discussed in the previous section. This can be assisted by the bidder's friends and associates[4] who 'warehouse' the target company equity prior to a bid. The majority of those acquirers who were interviewed agreed on the importance of warehousing, although one respondent was somewhat sceptical of the use of 'friends'. The advantage of pre-bid acquisitions of target equity as a source of dealing profit in the event of counter-bids was also stressed by a majority of the acquirers.

Various practices exist to control the bidder's share price. During bids it may be desirable to keep up the bidder's share price where the bid terms are largely in paper so that the value of the bid remains steady or so that a cash alternative is rendered less attractive. Again friends and associates can be helpful in promoting these manipulations. There was an impression from the respondents that a considerable business goes on behind the scenes in buying and selling shares between financially-oriented acquirers. (This is supported by the closely knit but changing interrelationships amongst F-type acquirer companies.)

In acquisitions of targets which are closely held and where as a result of the bid a sizeable proportion of acquirer equity falls into the hands of a few individuals there is the danger of the acquirer's equity share price being depressed during disposal of such equity blocks. In the case of private companies restrictive sale clauses are quite often made but for public company targets formal agreements are not feasible. Underwriting the bid for large target shareholders offers a further means of dispersing potentially sizeable blocks of acquirer equity.

The need to arrange market operations in advance inevitably requires information transmission amongst operators and their merchant bank advisers, friends and associates. Consequently as a warehouser there would seem to be opportunities to be friendly and make a profit at the same time.

Evidence from case studies. The offer documents issued in conjunction with bids for publicly quoted target companies state the pre-bid holdings of the acquirer company and of its associates in the target. If the bid is recommended by the target company directors then the offer document also gives details of their shareholdings in the target. Figure 4:2 summarizes this data for the bids by the case study acquirer companies A and B.

	Acquirer A				Acquirer B			
Deal	A–1	A–2	A–3	B–1	B–2	B–3	B–4	B–5
Target directors	40	31	11	33	–	12	–	0
Acquirer company	–	–	–	17	50	43	38	–
Acquirer's bankers	–	4	–	–	–	–	–	
Total	40	35	11	50	50	55	38	0

Notes: Bid B–2 was not an agreed bid. Acquirer B held 9% prior to its first offer and then bought further shares in the market.

Bid B–5 involved agreement with a third party which in fact controlled the target company prior to bid announcement.

Figure 4:2 Percentage holdings of target company equity at the date of the offer document by the case study acquirer companies

All bids except for B–2 were issued as agreed bids. In that case a counter-offer was made which could have yielded a dealing profit for acquirer B if it had not chosen to increase its offer and gain acceptance. Bid A–3, which had a a relatively low pre-bid holding by the acquirer, concerned the acquisition of a company which was making considerable losses and the offer document contained a strong recommendation for acceptance from the target company chairman. Figure 4:2 therefore indicates the extent of pre-bid support for the deals which except for B–2 precluded bids by third parties.

Formation of bid premiums

The process by which bid premiums were formed was suggested by analysis of results of interviews with experts. It was normal practice to gain maximal equity holdings in target companies prior to a bid and/or to gain approval of the bid terms from target company directors before announcing the bid. It is presumed that such an approval, when translated into a circular recommending the bid from the target company directors to the target company shareholders, makes the acceptance of the latter to the bid more likely.

Also equity held by the acquirer company in the target company prior to announcement of the bid would be expected to reduce the bid premium. Asset backing for the target company's share price was mentioned as a factor which affects the value of a bid in that the exit valuation of the target would be higher the higher was the asset value in relation to the pre-bid share price. Finally the bid premium would tend to be larger as the amount of equity consideration in the offer package is reduced; larger equity content in the package means that the target company shareholders gain from profits subsequently derived from the assets of their company so that a premium is of less importance. Figure 4:3 outlines the interrelationship of these concepts together with the impact of financial market constraints.

These considerations were tested against the data for the acquisitions of the case study companies. Figure 4:4 presents the data to which a linear regression model was fitted by ordinary least squares. The model took the form:

$$Y = A + BX_1 + CX_2 + DX_3 + e \qquad (4)$$

where Y is the bid premium % defined in Figure 3:5

X_1 is the % of target company equity held in total by the acquirer company, its merchant bankers and the target company directors (in agreed bids) and as shown in Figure 4:4

X_2 is the % of ordinary shares in the offer package as shown in Figure 4:4 ignoring any future equity rights attaching to convertible securities

X_3 is the target company assets backing dividend by its share price as shown in Figure 4:4

e is an error term.

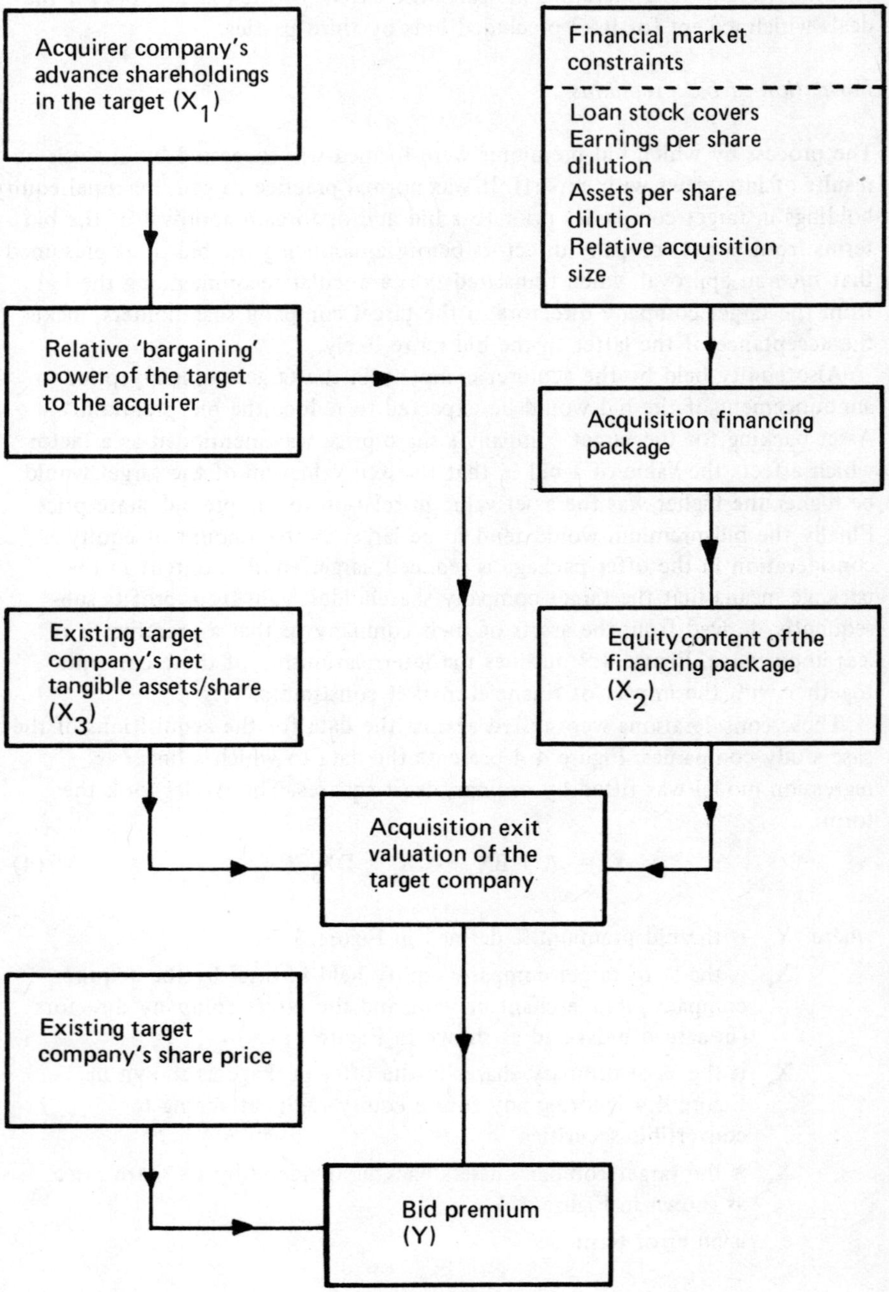

Figure 4:3 Formation of bid premiums

Acquirer company	Acquired company	Equity held in advance of first bid (X_1)	Equity content of acquisition package (X_2)	Net tangible assets/equity capitalization of target (A) (X_3)	Bid premium by way of capital value (B) (Y)
Acquirer A	A–1	40%	26%	180.0%	93%
	A–2	35%	30%	144.0%	57% (average)
	A–3	11%	30%	141.8%	13%
Acquirer B	B–1	50%	100%	195.8%	10%
	B–2	9%	29%	168.0%	230%
	B–3	55%	36%	223.4%	98%
	B–4	38%	36%	208.6%	87%
	B–5	0%	14%	87.0%	120% (approx)

Notes: (A) Based upon target company share prices approximately two months prior to public announcement of the bid (to avoid the effects of leakage of information) and using most up-to-date estimates of property valuations from offer documents.

(B) Calculated from the share exchange exit valuation excess over the acquired firm's share price two months prior to the date of the first bid as a percentage of the latter.

Figure 4:4 Bid premiums: bargaining aspects

The results are shown below together with the regression coefficient $\bar{R}^2$

Regression results – values and significance

A	B	C	D	$\bar{R}^2$
5.17	–3.72	–1.44	1.55	0.85

adjusted for degrees of freedom; t-test results for the coefficients A, B, C, D showed that for B, C, D they were significant at the 5% confidence level whereas the coefficient of A was insignificant. Although the limited number of observations preclude any definitive result, the fitted values have their signs in the hypothesized directions and coefficients which do not seem implausible. The results infer that the bid premium falls as the advance equity rises and as the equity content of the bid rises, but rises as the asset backing in relation to the pre-bid share price of the target rises. Bargaining power which is identified primarily with X_1 has the most important influence upon the bid premium.

It is likely that the acquirer companies' expectations of gains from these acquisitions were higher than those of the targets partly because of the rationalization expertise of the former and partly because of their access to better opportunities for redeployment of assets. For such circumstances the Stapleton model implies that the acquirers would want to offer non-equity consideration, subject to financial market constraints which have been presented for the same acquisitions in Figure 3:5. The importance of bargaining power, the relatively low equity content of the bids and the signs of the coefficients fitted to the above model are all complementary to Stapleton's bargaining model.

Company law and market operations

No illegal practices were located during the course of the research. Market operations and some inferences about accounting for acquisitions, however, allow actions which go against what one might regard as the spirit of the city as suggested by the City Code on Takeovers and Mergers (1974) (although not in instances of the acquisitions made by the case study companies). It is worth considering briefly the effects of market operations and why they cannot be pinpointed under present circumstances.

Successful market operations result from wielding power in the stock market which is in excess of normal, perfectly competitive forces. If a target company's equity is held in sufficient quantity to force a lower acquisition exit valuation than might arise in perfectly competitive market conditions then there would tend to be a transfer of wealth from the target equity holders in total to the acquirer company shareholders. To what extent this wealth is distributed evenly to the acquirer and the acquired firms' original shareholders after the bid depends upon offer package content. If as suggested by the bid premium model the exercise of market power reduces the equity given by the acquirer to the acquired firm's shareholders then the effect of market operations is to transfer wealth from the acquired firm's shareholders to the acquirer shareholders in excess of that which would have been transferred by the same acquisition under perfectly competitive stock markets.

There is another side to this coin, namely that to do the forcing there must be some gain to the market operators who buy pre-bid target equity. Either they must buy it because they would not otherwise have done so and therefore would have made no profit if they had not known about the potential bid or they participate in other gains as a result of the acquisition. Such other gains may include investment management, underwriting, arrangement of finance, or holding of acquirer company equity. From the acquirer company's viewpoint purchases by third parties of target equity prior to a bid will be advantageous provided there is a suitable trade-off between increased negotiating force for agreement of attractive bid terms and the marginal pre-bid rise in target equity due to such purchases. The target company shareholders could benefit from such a rise due to these purchases even if the bid did not ultimately materialize.

Whether an investment in a company prior to a bid is a market operation or a pure investment is difficult to expose, especially if investment management is the normal business of the investor. This would of course be the case for firms which run investment or unit trusts, pension funds or insurance companies. Thus the scope for legal exercise of market power is extensive and a perfectly rational aid to creating wealth. If the company which pursues market operations is also one which is subject to reduced disclosure requirements under the 1967 Companies Act then its position is that much more flexible.

Whilst stressing the legality and normal profit-seeking motives of market operations, there is the social question of whether instrusions which could detract from the competitive nature of UK stock markets are acceptable. Emotive issue that this currently is, it nevertheless deserves objective research to clarify the picture before either legal steps are taken to penalize currently legal and rational operations which may not cause market imperfections or they are not taken when they should be if democratic values so demand.

One should not forget however that there are strong arguments as to the commercial benefits which F-type acquirer companies can bring. For example how much longer might their acquisition targets have remained viable without takeover? Would more jobs have been lost without the takeover than consequent upon it? Does not F-type takeover release resources to more profitable and efficient uses? The high equity stakes of directors of F-type companies in their firms involves them directly in bearing financial responsibility for the results of their decisions. This contrasts with many large UK firms where executives are often not major shareholders and can perform commercially badly for many years without being shaken up or without suffering personal capital loss.

Consequently one may plead for considered judgment based on sound research rather than emotively-based political decisions concerning aspects of public policy towards financially-oriented acquisition activity.

Selection of financing instruments

The variety of financing instruments available to companies is extensive, reflecting both legal rights for securities and methods of profit distribution. At first sight one might expect there to be individual valuation bases for each different type of investment but in fact valuation of company securities can be categorized into a single conceptual framework. This section first discusses the framework for valuation of corporate securities and then examines the implications for acquisition financing strategy.

Interrelated nature of valuations

Fixed-interest borrowings of a company include mortgages, secured loan stock, unsecured loan stock, preference shares and bank overdrafts. Between fixed-interest borrowing and ordinary shares lie mixed securities such as convertible loans, loans with warrants and convertible preference shares. Each of these has a particular risk-and-return profile which is continuously adjusted as a result of investors attempting to maximize the utility of their individual portfolios. If one regards a company as a collection of income-producing assets financed by some combination of fixed-interest stock and equity then the equity holders may be considered to hold an option on the assets of the company which up to some nominal value of the fixed-interest securities belong to the debt holders and any excess over that level is attributable to the shareholders. Convertible loan stock may be split into two components, one being a straight loan stock and the other a subscription right or warrant linked to the equity in the company. The value of a warrant per equity share of a company cannot be negative nor less than the actual price of an equity share minus the price at which the warrant is exercisable (together with any subscription cost). These ideas have been propounded by Black and Scholes (1973) and by Merton (1973) who show that equity shares are effectively infinite-dated warrants with a zero exercise price. The interrelated valuations of the various financing instruments in relation to company assets are indicated in Figure 4:5.

Lines A, B, C, D in Figure 4:5 (B) indicate the value of warrants with successively shorter maturities; line A is the 45° line for a warrant of infinite maturity and zero exercise price. At a conceptual level therefore the whole of a company's securities can be regarded as a combination of company assets and warrants of various maturities and exercise prices into the assets. Direct translation of these concepts into practical valuation models is infeasible as Black and Scholes point out and furthermore implies some intrinsic worth for

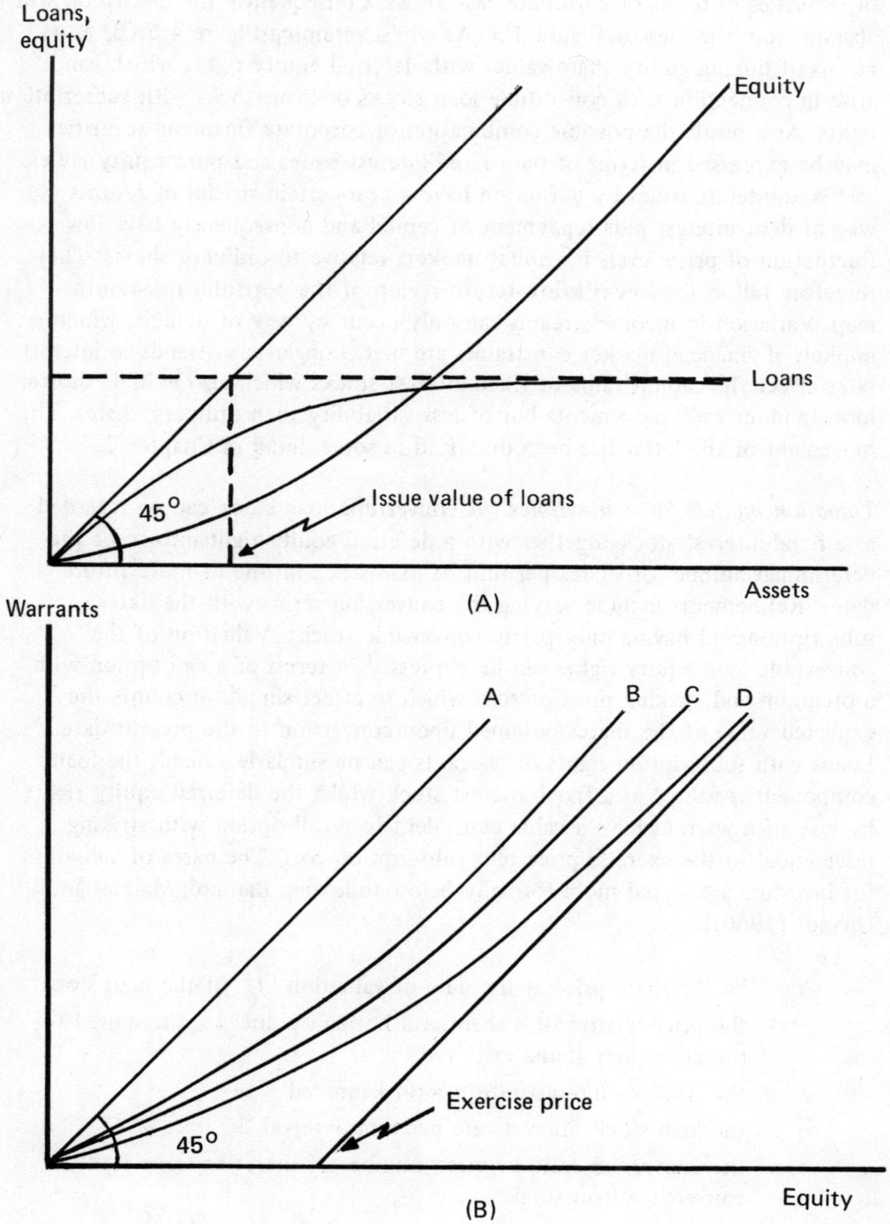

Figure 4:5 Financing instrument values relative to company assets

the company's assets. The latter runs against much of the discussion of security market price movement research which is concerned with the trading of company securities between marginal buyers and sellers rather than absolute valuation of securities in terms of corporate cash flows. Consequently the discussion will abstain from the idea of Figure 4:5 (A) whilst retaining Figure 4:5 (B) as a means of linking equity share values with deferred equity rights which can arise in connection with convertible loan stocks or loan stocks with subscription rights. As a result the possible combination of corporate financing securities may be expressed in terms of pure fixed-interest issues and pure equity issues.

Fixed-interest issues by definition have a near-certain stream of returns by way of debt interest plus repayment of capital and consequently have low fluctuation of price levels in capital markets relative to ordinary shares. They therefore fall in the low-risk/low-return region of the portfolio risk-return map. Variation in income streams can only occur by way of default, which is unlikely if financial market constraints are met. Longer-term trends in interest rates affect the capital value of fixed-interest stocks which also exhibit shorter-term random walk movements but of less variability than ordinary shares. The movement of the latter has been discussed in some detail in Chapter 2.

Valuation models for convertibles. A convertible loan stock can be regarded as a fixed-interest stock together with a deferred equity right into some predetermined number of shares per unit of loan stock at one or more future dates. Refinements include varying the conversion terms with the dates of subscription and having only partly convertible stocks. Valuation of the convertible loan equity rights can be expressed in terms of a call option with a premium and striking price of zero which in effect simply discounts the expected value of the shares obtained upon conversion to the present date. Loans with subscription rights or warrants can be similarly valued; the loan component is valued as a fixed-interest stock whilst the deferred equity rights by way of a warrant have a value equivalent to a call option with striking price equal to the exercise price plus subscription cost. The bases of valuation for investors are stated more formally below following Baumol, Malkiel and Quandt (1966).

Let

- Y_0 be the share price at the date of valuation t_0 of the loan stock
- $y(t)$ the price-relative of a share at a horizon point t, discounted to present values at the rate r
- r the risk-free interest rate per time interval
- q the loan stock interest rate per time interval
- c the conversion ratio between number of shares and one unit of convertible loan stock
- p the proportion of the loan stock which is convertible
- w the number of shares available for subscription to the holder of a unit of loan stock carrying subscription rights

E	the exercise price for subscription rights
Q	the cash subscription required per share
P	the present value of the loan stock
h	the conversion/subscription date in unit time intervals ahead
N	the nominal value of the loan stock
B	the loan stock's pure bond equivalent value
$f(y, t_0)$	is the distribution of the share price-relative at the horizon point t which may be affected by the current time t_0 at which the loan stock is valued.

The straight loan equivalent value B is simply a discounted valuation of its repayments by interest and capital. If held to maturity

$$B = \sum_{i=1}^{h} \frac{qN}{(1+r)^i} + \frac{N}{(1+r)^h}$$

(If not held to maturity then the terminal receipt will be probabilistic and based upon market prices; even if held to maturity there is strictly a probabilistic valuation problem linked to risk of default.)

Assuming B is constant over a period of time then Baumol, Malkiel and Quandt arrive at valuations for values of a convertible loan stock in terms of its equity equivalent value and its bond equivalent value, respectively

$$P_1 \geqslant Y_0 pc + \int_0^{B/Y_0 pc} f(y, t_0)[pB - y(t)Y_0 pc] \, dy(t) \quad \text{wrt equity value} \qquad (5)$$

$$P_2 \geqslant B + \int_{B/Y_0 pc}^{\infty} f(y, t_0)[y(t)Y_0 pc - pB] \, dy(t) \quad \text{wrt bond value} \qquad (6)$$

$$P = \text{Max}(P_1, P_2)$$

In the case of the loan stock which carries subscription rights, the latter are valueless at maturity when the expected equity price lies below (E + Q). Since investors hold both the loan stock and the warrant the value of the loan with subscription rights is given by one expression analogous to (6) above.

$$P \geqslant B + \int_{(E+Q)/Y_0}^{\infty} f(y, t_0)[y(t)Y_0 w] \, dy(t) \qquad (7)$$

Loan stock values therefore reflect the probabilistic nature of the ordinary share price y and valuation necessitates making *a priori* judgments on f(y) for a given horizon point in time. The distribution of y implicitly assumes that the amount of equity capital in issue is not materially altered as a result of conversion or exercise of subscription rights. If the alteration is material then the relevant distribution of y will differ from that of the share price prior to conversion or subscription and would need to be expressed in terms of total equity which includes shares and warrants outstanding; the point is amplified by Black and Scholes[5]. Additional reality may be introduced into the models by acknowledging possible variations in r over a period of time consistent with the term structure of interest rates.

Equity issues and deferred rights

The acquisition-financing decision involves several groups of investors. The acquirer company shareholders prior to the bid must not be made worse off in a portfolio sense as a result of the bid. The portfolio attractions of the combined company securities post-bid should be better than that of the acquirer company securities pre-bid in order for its capitalization to rise as a result of marginal net investment demand. Strict application of Levy and Sarnat's argument, that in the absence of joint operating economies an acquisition does not benefit shareholders, may be relaxed to some extent by the tax advantages of moving to a superior debt:equity financing ratio, the reduction of risk to lenders by way of insolvency possibilities and cost savings in fund raising[6]; such changes will of themselves add to the portfolio attractions of the combined equity vis-à-vis its component parts for investors without holdings in either of the combining companies. Finally shareholders in the target company must be bought out by a combination of a sufficiently attractive offer package and negotiation procedures.

Trade-off between deferred equity rights and cost of straight debt. The discussion in Chapter 3 implied that the three groups of investors, namely target shareholders, acquirer shareholders and potential future shareholders, would be satisfied provided financial market constraints were met. The model of financial market constraints is a short-term ('satisficing') model which does not consider the longer-term impact of equity dilution in the acquirer company by way of deferred equity rights. Evidently the acquirer shareholders have an interest in minimizing the present value of these rights whereas the target company shareholders will wish to maximize the value. The acquirer company will generally wish to maximize the fixed interest and cash content of a bid package and could therefore regard the disadvantage of the future equity rights as the equivalent means of paying the difference between the lower coupon of a loan stock which carries equity rights and the market rate on a straight loan stock. In other words the equity attachments of a loan stock provide a way of satisfying financial market constraints alternative to the issue of straight debt and equity. Denoting the interest rate on straight debt by s, the value of a straight debt loan D with the same nominal value N and held to maturity at the horizon h is:

$$D = \sum_{i=1}^{h} \frac{sN}{(1+r)^i} + \frac{N}{(1+r)^h}$$

so that the value gained in interest payments by the acquirer company as a result of issuing a loan with equity conversion or subscription rights will be (8) below:

$$D = B = \sum_{i=1}^{h} \frac{(s-q)N}{(1+r)^i} \tag{8}$$

which should be set against the present value of the expected equity rights of the loan stock, assuming that the content of straight equity in the acquisition-financing package remains constant. For the convertible case the equity rights are the integral component of (6) so that for the convertible to be advantageous as against issue of straight debt

$$\sum_{i=1}^{h} \frac{(s-q)N}{(1+r)^i} > \int_{B/Y_0 pc}^{\infty} f(y, t_0)\,[y(t)Y_0 pc - pB]\; dy(t)$$

and for a loan stock with subscription rights

$$\sum_{i=1}^{h} \frac{(s-q)N}{(1+r)^i} > \int_{(E+Q)/Y_0}^{\infty} f(y, t_0)\,[y(t)Y_0 w]\; dy(t)$$

The decision variables involved are therefore p, c, q, h for the convertible and q, E, Q, h for the loan with subscription rights. For the convertible the acquirer will want to minimize p and c for a given $(s-q)$. In the case of the loan with equity subscription rights the acquirer will want to minimize w and maximize $(E+Q)$ for a given $(s-q)$. Thus a high exercise price and level of subscription will reduce the value of the warrants. The choice of h is not clear-cut and depends on the likely movements of share price relatives over a period of time. Both increasing trend and variability of share prices will be beneficial to holders of the deferred equity rights and consequently detrimental so far as dilution of equity holdings is concerned for existing shareholders in the issuing company. As discussed in Chapter 2, the stable Paretian model of price movements implies that as the distance of the horizon point n periods ahead increases the distribution mean increases in direct proportion to n and the variability measure c increases so that for a characteristic exponent a

$$c_n = n^{1/a} c$$

If, as appears to be generally true, $1.6 \leqslant a \leqslant 2.0$ then the ratio c_n/c increases with n but at a decreasing rate. Some trade-off will therefore exist between the rate of discount and the rate at which variability expands over a period of time; the latter being determined by a . Figure 4:6 plots graphs for the function

$$\frac{n^{1/a}}{(1+r)^n} \tag{9}$$

which reflects the interaction of the relative variability c_n/c and the discount multiplier $(1+r)^{-n}$. Curves are shown for r at 5%, 10%, 15%, 20% with $a = 2.0$ which is the normal distribution. Values of $a < 2.0$ will push the curves up and to the right. In the early stages of the life of a security the variability effect dominates whereas later on the compounding of the discount rate has a greater impact. Therefore an acquirer company wishing to issue loan stock with equity rights but to minimize the dilution consequences should either issue a stock with very distant equity rights so that the discount effect dominates in valuation of the deferred equity content, or have a small convertible proportion in the early years which is allowed to increase later, or use a stock with subscription rights which are set high relative to early share price movement expectations. It might even be possible to combine longer-term conversion rights with short-term warrant terms that make subscription unlikely until their present value becomes negligible. If the distribution of share prices is substantially non-normal with a well below 2.0 then longer-term subscription rights may become relatively valuable since the numerator will dominate the denominator in (9) for quite some time, especially if r is relatively low. If the amount of straight equity, ie ordinary shares, issued as part of the acquisition package is reduced by virtue of including loan stock with equity rights as opposed to straight loan stock then (8) would need to include the value of such a saving on the left-hand side. If the saving was a proportion m of the number of shares which would have been issued with a unit of straight loan stock, then the additional term required on the left-hand side of (8) would be the expected net present value of the proportion of shares which do not need to be issued:

$$\int_0^\infty Y_0 m\, f(y, t_0) y(t)\, dy(t)$$

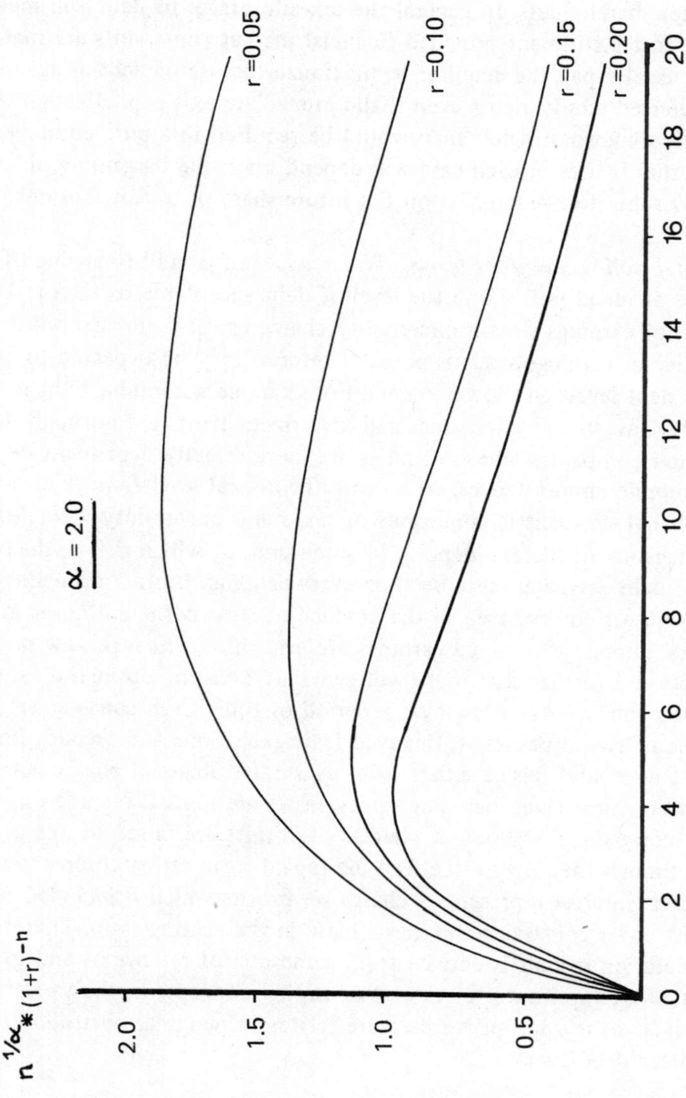

Figure 4:6 Interaction of variability in share prices and the discount rate in valuation of deferred equity rights

The acquirer's existing shareholders and future investors will benefit from achieving an overall minimum capitalization of the financing package (in the sense of minimum net present value of future cash outflows) rather than of any single component; however the bargaining process may well include consideration of the various instruments in separation especially as they will normally be quoted independently in the market and sale of them offers a way out for ex-target shareholders. In general the tax advantages of debt will make it the lowest cost instrument provided financial market constraints are met. Thus it will usually pay the acquirer to maximize the use of debt as against equity and deferred equity rights even if the immediate exit capitalization of the target is somewhat higher than would be required in a pure equity exchange. The actual figures in each case will depend upon the bargaining process and *a priori* subjective judgments on the future share price distributions.

Dividend policy and debt levels. Wider issues of overall financing of the firm involve dividend policy and the level of debt acceptable to the market in respect of earnings stream uncertainty characteristics; in other words lower volatility of earnings streams pre-debt interest may be expected to allow higher debt levels and lower covers. For example acceptable debt levels in property investment companies and investment trusts are normally higher than for other companies whose earnings are more directly dependent on fluctuations in economic circumstances. At a more theoretical level Lintner (1962) has argued that, in realistic conditions of taxes and uncertainty, debt levels are advantageous to shareholders up to some limit at which risk of default and related debt servicing costs become overwhelming. Lintner also shows that new issues of equity, even in the absence of issue costs, are never in shareholders' interest if retained earnings are available to finance new investment projects and further that there will generally be some optimal dividend path for the company to follow over a period of time. Cash consideration in bids may be of two types: first, financed from retentions and second, financed by way of new fund raising either from overdrafts, loans or equity issues. For acquisition financing, loan and equity issues are normally made direct to target company shareholders whereas overdrafts are raised by the acquirer (even though they may effectively be repaid from target company assets). Overdraft interest represents a charge on profits which is included in the interest cover constraint and an increase in the gearing ratio. Therefore cash consideration in bids is derived from some mix of retentions and overdrafts; whilst it is tempting to relate cost of capital concepts to the various financing instruments the appropriate measure relates to marginal portfolio consequences as indicated in Chapter 2.

Capital rationing circumstances

Some brief comments are in order for circumstances where a company has limited access to funds. Unquoted companies are perhaps the most obvious examples in that equity consideration is frequently not acceptable as acquisition consideration and therefore loans or overdrafts are the prime methods for acquisition financing. The disadvantages of equity consideration from the acquirer's viewpoint include the possibilities of loss of some control over the combined companies, implicit commitment to a public quotation at a future date, additional estate duty problems, intrusion of third parties at board level etc. From the viewpoint of target company shareholders, minority unquoted holdings have poor realizability prospects, difficult valuation problems, lack of opportunities for control of a private company's affairs, possible tax drawbacks etc.

Reducing the possibilities of equity financing for a policy of growth by acquisition does not invalidate the model of financial constraints but it clearly does restrict the range of feasible solutions for given constraint levels on loan stock and overdraft financing. Indeed the constrained financing model is a model for capital rationing situations in which companies find it hard or prohibitively expensive to raise finance once constraints are breached. Unquoted companies are by definition prevented from adopting an investment portfolio risk-return viewpoint based upon quoted share prices, so it is not immediately obvious what criterion should be used to evaluate acquisition opportunities.

The problem has been approached by Baumol and Quandt (1965) who assume an investor utility function for a stream of withdrawals from the company. (These withdrawals could be a series of dividend flows or flows of salaries plus dividends or salaries plus terminal value etc.) Overall the shareholder objective function takes the form of a maximization of utility of the stream of withdrawals from the company subject to financing limitations. This is the analogous unquoted company objective function to that for quoted companies, namely shareholder net present wealth maximization which implies maximization of the current share price in a portfolio context. Strictly the unquoted situation should include the effects of shareholders' other investments. The recourse to a specific utility function emphasizes the fact that the decision-maker in an unquoted situation is dealing for his own particular set of preferences over a period of time and must define them subjectively before reaching decisions; an alternative approach for unquoted company situations is to assume that the company was quoted and to estimate its capitalization in the stock market from comparison with similar companies that are quoted. In the contrasting quoted company situation the decision criterion can be found objectively from consideration of the effect of an acquisition on investors' portfolios in the securities market, given the assumptions underlying portfolio theory which have been mentioned in Chapter 2.

Acquisition financing from an unquoted acquirer vehicle requires the shareholders to assess exactly what level of risk they are prepared to bear, not necessarily only from limited liability shareholdings but also by way of personal guarantees etc, in order to push available finance beyond loan stock cover limits. Guarantees beyond company funds may be regarded as contingent equity claims by the company upon its shareholders. Conceptually the financing institution, generally a bank, puts up money over and above accepted banking criteria for the company alone against personal securities of value equal to the expected cost of default in excess of company funds. The latter 'value' is a utility of money measure for the company shareholder. The private company shareholder could give away equity in the company to a financing institution to avoid this personal risk; indeed financial institutions such as ICFC offer exactly this kind of facility whilst leaving voting control in the hands of the existing shareholders. The risk-bearing choice is fairly stark for expansion-minded and unquoted companies: either expand within retained earnings facilities and loans/overdrafts available to the company on its own or, if greater expansion is desired, undertake personal risk-bearing of an unlimited nature to extend financing facilities, or bring a financing partner into the equity base in exchange for limited personal risk-bearing.

The question arises as to whether a financially-oriented acquisition policy necessarily requires a quoted vehicle. The main reasons for using a quoted vehicle would seem to be:

1 There is a minimum size of target company in which it is worthwhile to invest expertise in realization and rationalization. Such an acquisition may be hard to finance without a quoted equity base.
2 Quoted equity can be used as an acquisition instrument both directly and as a means of providing deferred equity rights in convertible loans and loans with subscription rights.
3 Wealth can be more readily realized through a quoted company.
4 Market operations can reduce acquisition cost.

Against these factors the advantages of growth from an unquoted vehicle are:

1 There is less dependence on investor approval and stock market fluctuations.
2 Any equity issue is a dilution in existing shareholder interests; consequently there are grounds for making higher value cash offers for a target company to avoid giving away subsequent equity growth.
3 The essence of an F-type acquirer's success is the taking of investment opportunities which offer rationalization and cash realization prospects. Imposition of additional funding constraints such as lack of equity or convertible loan issues tightens up the available opportunities for acquisition but keeps the equity base intact.

The speed of growth in shareholder wealth is likely to be a function of available finance and available investment opportunities. Faster growth through increased availability of finance and thus feasible investment opportunities is like to be achieved at the expense of equity dilution.

Summary

The formation of bid premiums is interrelated with selection of financing instruments and with bargaining between acquirer company and target company representatives.

It has been argued that circumstances exist where bid premiums are not logically necessary although in most cases a premium will be required to interest target company shareholders in an acquisition. The bargaining process involves parties who may hold differing expectations about the future and who may benefit from influencing expectations of the other party either up or down. Relative bargaining strength may be promoted by the use of market operations to increase the potential acquirer company's holdings of target company equity capital. Agreement of acquisition terms with directors and/or major shareholders of the target prior to publication of the bid tends to reduce the bid premium which might otherwise be necessary. Motivations of directors different from those of their shareholders will tend to benefit the other bargaining party in arranging acquisition terms. The negotiated terms reflect selection of financing instruments. Larger bid premiums will tend to occur where there is a lower equity content in the bid.

The use of convertible loans and loans which carry deferred equity rights can be evaluated as mixtures of straight loan stock and values of pure equity holdings. Subjective probability distributions of future share price relatives must be formed to value the latter. There are trade-offs to make between the discount rate and share price volatility which will affect the value of deferred equity rights. The acquirer company has the opportunity to select the parameters of the deferred equity rights in a manner advantageous to itself, depending upon the efficiency of valuation in financial markets for convertibles and loans with subscription rights.

References

1 Granger and Morgenstern (1970), Chapter 1, discuss this important issue at greater length.

2 Baumol (1962) and Williamson (1967) make this point based upon e empirical evidence from research studies, particularly the latter.

3 The City Code on Takeovers and Mergers (1974) has an influence on this matter. The requirement for cash alternatives under the 15% rule is a matter for consideration in practical situations. Without a bid being made it would be possible to buy up to 40% which in effect would create opportunities for blocking of deals. The 1967 Companies Act disclosure rule on holdings of 10% or more is a further relevant factor.

4 Only the more widely practised market operations are discussed in the text. The definition of an associate is given in the City Code (above).

5 Black and Scholes (1973), pp. 648-9, advance the formulation of option prices from the model of Baumol, Malkiel and Quandt (1966). However the latter has been used as a basis for discussion in the text since Black and Scholes assume a model of share price movements which does not fit well with the stable non-normal approximation to observed share price changes.

6 See Levy and Sarnat (1970).

5

Search and Evaluation

Introduction

A successful policy of growth by external investment requires access to adequate acquisition opportunities and competent appraisal of the advantages and disadvantages of each proposition. Within feasible bounds of cost and time, a company which aims to pursue a policy of growth by acquisition needs to effectively direct its methods for receipt of information about potential target companies. Given sufficient proposals for acquisition, the company must establish its acquisition objectives and criteria for evaluating potential target companies which are consistent with those objectives. The process of proposing and evaluating acquisitions is a continuing task in which the criteria and values of the criteria are likely to change as the acquirer company develops from previous acquisitions. The adaptive nature of growth by pursuit of an active acquisition policy requires procedures for continuous monitoring of information about target companies together with analytic capabilities for reaching decisions at various and often sudden intervals.

The discussion in this chapter aims to bring aspects of the existing business literature on search processes together with research results pertaining to F-type acquisition activity in order to build models for acquisition search and evaluation procedures which have descriptive and possibly prescriptive content. As with the preceding chapters, the emphasis is upon financial strategy but other non-financial factors could be incorporated into the subsequent analytic framework.

Indications from business literature

There is a large number of papers and texts in the business management literature concerning how to seek out potential acqusition target companies, how to negotiate with target managements and how to frame bid terms. For example a company aiming to make acquisitions is advised to build up a set of criteria against which to evaluate proposed targets. These criteria are related to a unique profile of factors about the existing state and resources of the company. The ideas of 'fit charts' and checklists for use by acquirer companies which are outlined in numerous books and articles imply a process of matching up resources and attributes of potential business combinations. Vance (1969) indicates a number of financial and non-financial factors which would make a company a potentially attractive acqusition target: these include high liquidity, low debt, low P/E ratio, stable earnings and, amongst non-financial factors, dominant market position, being in a growth industry and being a link in the vertical or horizontal integration plan of another company. Kitching (1967) and others emphasize the need for interconsistency of the various criteria and rigorous application of those that are regarded as crucial in locating and negotiating a suitable combination. Taylor (1970) has flow-charted the acquisition task into a sequence of steps and detailed outlines of the personnel involved.

Specific constraints upon possible acquisitions are frequently mentioned; Linowes (1968) includes acquisition size, growth rate, valuation and managerial and business fit stated within acceptable limits in recognition that the boundaries between the criteria are probably inter-dependent and need to be flexible. These rather general criteria would be used as an initial screening device. Earnings stability, market dependence, ownership diffusion and competitive position have also been proposed by Wyatt and Kieso (1969) as screening criteria.

The emphasis of the prescriptive literature is therefore upon formalized rational search and analysis of prospective acquisitions. Relatively little attention is paid to opportunistic, time-constrained decision-making in the evaluation of acquisition proposals. The limitations placed upon the amount of search activity due to cost considerations and the extent of sources of information available to individual firms is not generally considered. The external appraisal process of Ansoff (1968) would provide a highly comprehensive analysis if carried out in practice but would involve considerable staff time and effort; nor is it explicitly a dynamic model. Whilst valuable as a developed static framework, it is unlikely to be a suitable description of the more entrepreneurial and flexible search processes which are associated with F-type acquisition activity.

Descriptive – goals and search procedures

Parts of the more academic literature contribute to the concept of an acquisition search process. In particular the behavioural theory of the firm which is based upon the ideas of organizational goals, expectations and choice describes 'problem-directed' search processes as a part of the decision-making process of an organization. The concept of organizational goals outlined by Cyert and March (1963) comprises a list of goals coupled with an aspiration level for each goal. Goals and subgoals may be seen as the criteria which firms set up for search and negotiations; aspiration levels indirectly relate to the weightings attached to each criteria. For example a financially (goal)-oriented acquirer is likely to attach greater importance to asset realizability in a potential target company than an industrially (goal)-oriented acquirer. Cyert and March suggest that organizational goals are subject to continuing change and represent at any time the interests of various coalitions within the firm.

Similar thinking is displayed by Mackintosh (1963) in the notion of 'boundary conditions' within which firms operate and which may arise from a combination of internal ideology of management and externally imposed environmental features. Firms can actively seek to change the conditions which limit their development in course of time towards the firm's goals. The notion of 'node commonality' of Narver (1967) as applied to organizational activities is a similar concept: high node commonality between prospective combining partners would be associated with a high degree of fit or potential synergy between the combining firms' resources. The concern in much of the behavioural theory of the firms' literature with 'problem-solving' is a somewhat introverted view by firms of their changing activity; in contrast the work of Penrose (1966) is more concerned with opportunistic behaviour. It is suggested that these types of managerial behaviour form two ends of a continuous spectrum; for example market share protection may be seen as problem solving whereas the financially-oriented asset realization and rationalization activities of some entrepreneurial acquiring companies conform more to an opportunistic behavioural mode.

The adaptive nature of the business environment suggests that the motives for acquisition are likely to vary widely both amongst different bidders and over a period of time. This is recognized by Penrose, particularly in her discussion of a firm which, through expansion by internal and external means, becomes progressively more like an investment trust. Penrose suggests that the appropriate means of analysis of growth for an industrial firm concerned with organizing production and distribution is likely to differ from that appropriate to analysis of growth of a primarily financial institution, the distinguishing boundary being related to the type of organizational structure and objectives and modes of communication within the firm.

Sources of information

Acknowledging that the real environment is one of imperfect information and that business combination decisions are taken sometimes on quite slender (but not necessarily inadequate) analysis, the channels through which information passes to top executives may be of considerable importance in identifying potential combining companies. Although the search activity requires only one party it often involves professional assistance from other parties and in some cases the other parties, such as merchant bankers, may have the prime function in promoting and creating a combination. The merchant banking firms are in many cases still largely owned and/or managed by closely knit families and furthermore many merchant bankers hold directorships of quoted companies, in particular those for whom they act as merchant bankers. Consequently and deliberately merchant bankers are closely informed about their clients' affairs and are often consulted on important strategic decisions.

Similar considerations to a lesser extent apply to the accountants, stockbrokers, solicitors and clearing bankers of a firm. These professional advisers build up contacts and kinship relations amongst themselves; a trace of family connections of top decision-makers by Lupton and Wilson (1959) shows that some of the familiar merchant banking families are connected by kinship as well as having joint business roles and similar educational backgrounds. It would not therefore be surprising if information relevant to mergers and acquisitions were transmitted through this network of well-connected people. The information transmission mechanisms and types of information used by managers in various business environments has been studied in some depth by Aguilar (1967). His study provides a framework within which to place the preceding discussion of personal contacts and professional advisers who may act as data sources to firms.

Aguilar considers three aspects of information receipt by managers in companies: first what information they obtain, second from what sources they obtain it, and third how they obtain it. Regarding the first aspect his results suggested that most information received by line managers was about the product market and related primarily to the individual manager's functional speciality. Financial executives were the most likely to become involved in data about acquisition prospects and by implication least involved in day-to-day operating responsibilities. For the second aspect there was a heavy emphasis on personal contacts as sources of information rather than impersonal sources such as publications. Aguilar found that the more senior the executive the greater the emphasis that was placed upon personal contacts for information gathering as opposed to impersonal contacts. For the third aspect Aguilar split information received into solicited and unsolicited information. His results suggested that the information received by managers was evenly balanced between solicited and unsolicited information and that unsolicited information received from personal contacts tended to be directed mainly to topics of interest to individual managers. Aguilar's study is regarded as indicative rather than authoritative when applied to the topic of acquisition-search activity. It does serve however to support the importance of financial executives in acquisition-search processes and to imply that their contacts, who can direct relevant information about acquisitions to them, are likely to have an important role in creating acquisition opportunities. Trade contacts of product market managers may also form sources of data on acquisitions but these are likely to bear functional links with the managers' focal activities.

Practical sources. Sources of information can be both of a personal nature, such as individual contacts with marketing, production or financial managers, or of an impersonal nature such as technical, trade and financial publications and news media; however for the latter to become useful channels of information there must be someone who promotes an acquisition proposal based upon impersonal sources of information. Without attempting to provide an exhaustive directory of specific sources of information, the classification below serves to indicate the variety of information and sources which may be relevant for acquisition planning.

	Type of source	*Relevance*
(a)	IMPERSONAL	
	News media	General economic and social trends
	Financial press	Up-to-date company-specific reports. Reports on innovations, international and regional economies, share prices etc
	Legal and tax reports	Tax planning at national and international levels
	Trade and industry associations	Indication of technological changes, some company specific data, key personnel in the industry, company product ranges
	Extel and Moodies cards	Financial histories of companies, major shareholders, capital structures etc
	Stockbroker circulars	Assessment of company prospects, industry surveys, economic projections
	Government publications, white papers, trade reports	Financial and labour statistics, regional variations, consumer demand, investment intentions, special surveys, incentive grants, political intervention intentions
	International bodies	OECD, IMF, EEC publications and their equivalents are useful overall perspectives for international acquisition planning
	Company sales material and annual reports	Product range, marketing methods and channels, geographical area of operations, factory locations, employees, associate companies

(b) PERSONAL

Auditors/accountants	Experience with a variety of industries, tax information and planning
Bankers	Knowledge of possible acquisition targets, 'city' contacts, sources of finance, foreign exchange aspects
Merger brokers	Quantity of acquisition proposals, introductions, acquisition appraisal
Merchant bankers and stockbrokers	As for bankers but more specialized services, flotation and stock exchange procedures, placement of securities, acquisition advice and appraisal
Marketing staff	Knowledge of competitors, information about willing sellers, knowledge of firms with complementary products or areas of operations
Production and purchasing staff	Vertical integration to sources of supply, acquisition of competitor production facilities for scale economies. Knowledge of labour relations, production technology
Financial staff	Contacts with city personnel, analysis of target companies with complementary financial structures
Contacts with impersonal sources	Insight into relevant or impersonal source information
Estate agents	Knowledge of property assets of companies and valuation of development potential, location planning.

Financial model of the acquisition process

Interview and case study data has been noted in earlier chapters which supports the shareholder wealth maximization objective as a conceptual starting point for F-type acquirer company activity; the practical translation of this goal implied increased assets and earnings per share of the acquirer company as a result of acquisitions. From the financial market constraints model in Chapter 3 it is clear that the acquirer company's existing financial state and resources interact with this objective to define acquisition criteria, ie feasible regions for financial states of potential target companies. For example an acquirer company which has low net tangibles but excessive profits for debt principal and interest covers respectively suggests a need for added asset backing as opposed to additional earnings per share.

Dynamic context of acquisition activity

Interviews with experts suggested that the acquisition criteria in F-type acquirer companies were formed primarily by the chief executive in consultation with a few other key executives. (This is supported indirectly by the case study results which showed that the directors of F-type case study companies held significant equity stakes; they would therefore be rationally motivated to involve themselves closely in acquisition selection.) The interviews also suggested that F-type top executives matched the factors that they sought in target companies with the current financial and product market circumstances of their own companies. Of the acquirer executives who were interviewed, most had quite well-defined views as to the product markets in which they wished to be involved.

Some of the F-type companies had in effect inherited certain substantial industry sector activities and were diversifying from them along chosen paths, partly defined as a result of past acquisitions. Others had selected industries where the manufacturing commitments were relatively low; they were prepared to move into various industries meeting that constraint. It appeared that the range of industrial circumstances undertaken reflected the managerial resources which firms would bring to bear upon an acquisition as well as the acquisition objectives. If adequate industrial managerial skills exist then industrial choice becomes less crucial a constraint; on the other hand if the acquirer company has limited industrial management skills then the choice of industry is a more important constraint. An exception to the latter exists where the objective of the bid is asset realization and liquidation or sale of operating subsidiaries; this need not require extensive operating industrial management skills.

Interviews with experts showed that they tended to regard a particular F-type company as 'so and so's' company, run according to that particular person's objectives. Therefore it may be expected that changes in effective top management will alter objectives and strategy. However neither of the case study acquirer companies made material alterations to their boards of directors over the three-year period of acquisitions which was studied.

Not only will an acquisition by a particular acquirer company alter its overall state and resources as a result of former external (target company) resources becoming internal, but acquisitions and divestitures by third-party companies will affect the list of available target companies which may be screened for suitability as prospective acquisitions. The screening process, which is considered next, is regarded as a static process within the overall dynamic context in which acquisition growth occurs; the overall dynamic context is illustrated in Figure 5:1.

Figure 5:1 links the foregoing discussion together in a diagrammatic fashion. The existing situation for the acquirer company is shown to the left of the diagram as the basis for current acquisitions. Changes as a result of an acquisition then offer the basis for analysis of future acquisitions. Specifically the introduction of new top management as a result of an acquisition may affect the objectives of top management and therefore corporate strategy.

Introduction of formerly external resources to the acquirer company as a result of an acquisition will alter the resources and financial state of the acquirer.

Acquisition criteria are shown as resulting from the interaction of corporate strategy with existing resources and financial circumstances. Potential target companies would logically be screened against these acquisition criteria and purchase negotiations instigated with suitable target companies. The list of potential target companies will be affected by the actions of third parties such as other acquirer companies, consequently the list is likely to be changed frequently.

Static model of acquisition analysis

Figure 5:2 illustrates the overall model of acquisition analysis. The dashed box labelled 'screening' corresponds to the 'screening' box of Figure 5:1 and boxes marked 'existing strategic top management objectives', 'existing company strategy', 'existing resources and financial state' and 'acquisition criteria' correspond in both diagrams to indicate the linkage between them. Detailed comments on Figure 5:2 follows.

Sources of proposed target companies. The process of locating target companies was covered in interviews with experts. All the acquirer company executives who were interviewed agreed that the majority of proposals for acquisition come from internal research and this was corroborated by the merchant bankers. Nevertheless almost all the acquirer company executives mentioned merchant banks as important sources of target company proposals. It is worth repeating here that the F-type acquirer companies tended to be closely related to merchant banks by virtue of shareholdings, market operations and underwriting services; these relationships may be expected to generate a flow of information about acquisition prospects from merchant banks to target companies. Other sources mentioned were stockbrokers, internal management, trade contacts and merger brokers; the last mentioned were noted primarily for the volume of proposals. Information received from trade contacts and as a result of existing industrial commitments was thought to be rather more accurate and extensive than information about activities outside existing commitments. From these remarks it appears that an F-type acquirer is in the position of a recipient of information both as a result of internal research and as a result of external agents. Consequently the acquisition proposals can be opportunistic as well as the result of planned search activity.

Screening of target companies. The means of initial screening evidently requires some screening criteria which, it would be expected, would be consistent with subsequent, more detailed evaluation criteria. These criteria are discussed later but some indications of the process of initial screening were obtained. Experts mentioned that Extel and Moodies' cards were employed to review the financial and industrial state of potential target companies and that sometimes formalized checklists were used. (Appendix 4 contains a questionnaire designed to obtain information about a target company.) The respondents who mentioned the use of checklists were amongst the longer-established acquirers.

The idea of lists of prospective acquisition targets is in one sense a dynamic concept since opportunities arise in the course of time; however the static notion applicable to lists is that of appraising prospects during the intervals between any changes in acquirer state or strategy which would affect acquisition criteria. Therefore lists include any opportunities which have arisen during such an interval and the components of the list are then evaluated by screening. Revision of the list is a matter of definition; clearly a company which is acquired affects the list of available acquisition prospects for screening. Those acquirer company executives who were interviewed were asked whether they maintained continuing files on potential target companies which had been rejected as possible acquisitions at one point in time. For example the share prices of the potential acquirer and target companies could move relative to each other; a fall in target capitalization relative to that of the acquirer would make the acquisition that much easier for the acquirer whereas a relative rise would jeopardize the feasibility of acquisition from the acquirer company's viewpoint. Alternatively the target company might decide to realize some of its underutilized assets and thereby remove some of its attractions to potential acquirers. All the executives stated that continuing records were maintained since the grounds for rejection could alter in course of time. The revision of the pending list derives from the dynamic implications of the model as specificed in Figure 5:1.

The creation and subsequent flexibility of acquisition criteria was not researched in great detail; however the broad theme of the interview data suggested that criteria derived from top executives tended to become more formalized operationally as the acquirer developed. Flexibility of criteria for relaxation of constraint levels and the implicit urgency of the need to make acquisitions remain conjectural although the activity of the F-type companies and the thought that share rating is positively related to activity (see Chapter 3 under 'Evidence from case studies') do not conflict with the need to relax criteria if insufficient proposals arise. Figures 5:3 – 5:6 amplify the components of the screening process, namely prospect description, evaluation, assessment of financial constraints, and creation of an offer package.

Description and evaluation of prospective acquisition targets

The interview and case study evidence given in Chapter 3 supported the model of financial market constraints as a means of making acquisitions which would be favourable to investors. In financial terms these constraints make the formal link between financially-oriented acquisition strategy and the criteria against which prospective acquisitions can be assessed. Although it is only at the stage of negotiations that the financing package will tend to be finalized within financial market constraints, clearly there is little point in allowing

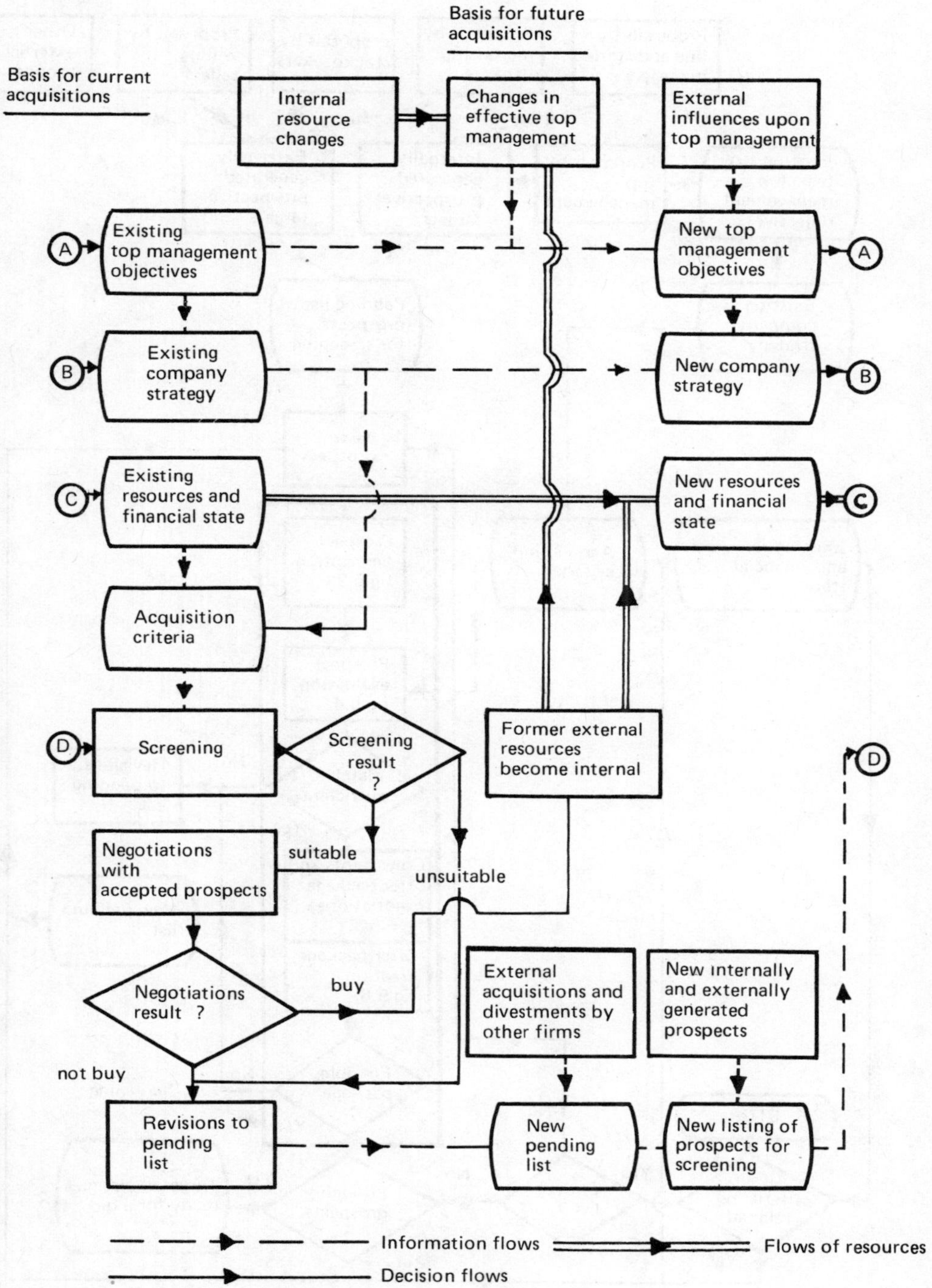

Figure 5:1 Dynamic context of acquisitions

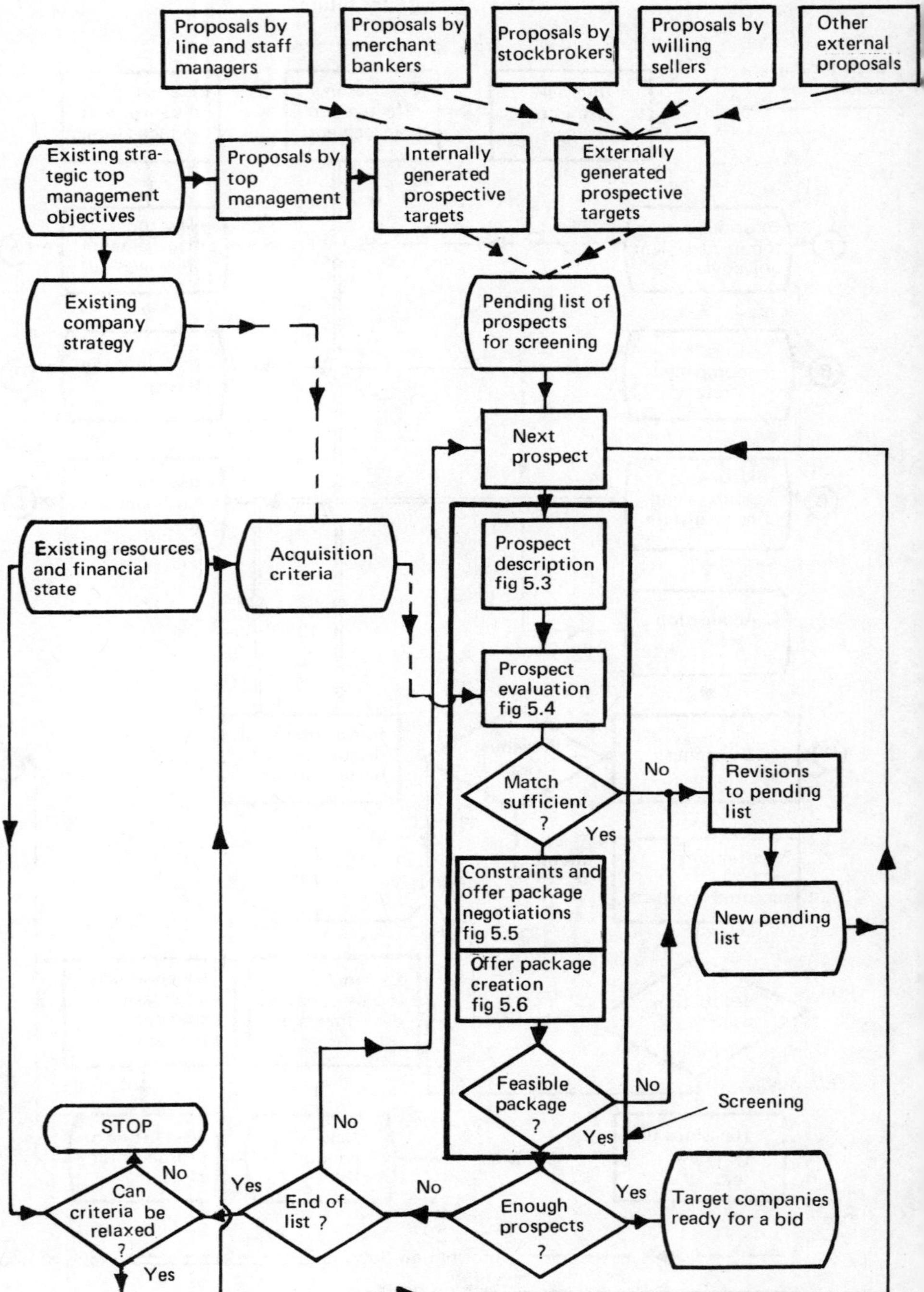

Figure 5:2 Static context of acquisitions

potential target companies through the screening stage unless they are likely to prove feasible acquisitions. Therefore the prospect description routine, outlined in Figure 5:3, emphasizes factors which are likely to promote additions to earnings and assets per share of the acquirer company.

Figure 5:3 is company rather than industry specific and implies that the acquirer company is primarily interested in what it can achieve from the target by way of realization of assets and rationalization of operating activities. Industry norms and past experience of acquirer executives serve as reference points for assessing potential performance. Interviews with acquirer executives suggested that they did not use formal industry comparative data to a great extent but tended to have a general feel for what constituted achievable rates of profit on sales and reasonable working capital requirements etc. (Thus the emphasis by Ansoff (1968) on industry search prior to company search may be somewhat inappropriate as a descriptive model of F-type acquirer activity in that industry data served only as a reference point for assessing what benefits could be achieved from an acquisition.)

Interviews and case study results indicated the importance of asset realizations. Indicators of surplus assets in target companies are provided by undervalued properties and sites which could be put to higher return usage, excessive working capital reflected in high levels of debtors and/or stocks to sales and spare-cash and near-cash assets such as marketable securities etc. However the latter are readily valued and therefore are unlikely to provide much scope for additional returns to an acquirer company. The rationalization opportunities from acquisition activity may be assessed by examining the operating ratios of the target, especially its cost structures in relation to sales, namely overhead costs:sales, gross margins:sales, labour cost:sales, employees:sales. In some cases these statistics may not be available and only net profit:sales can be determined. Additionally it may be possible to determine whether some divisions or product lines of the target have substantially differing profitabilities; situations where some divisions are highly profitable and some make substantial losses can offer excellent rationalization opportunities provided they are not interdependent and can be split up. The evidence from case studies and interviews indicated that these were the most important pieces of information about target company circumstances; each practical situation will give rise to many more questions of a detailed nature and the prospect description criteria can be extended to cover specific attributes which an acquirer company regards as important. Figure 5:3 is designed to capture the main areas for potential improvement in the returns from the target company. These may be described as a vector $\mathbf{A}$ whose elements are unity or zero depending upon whether each criterion offers scope or no scope for improvement respectively. The overall attractions of each target company could be described, from a prescriptive viewpoint, by a product of the vector $\mathbf{A}$ and a vector of weights $\mathbf{W}$ attaching to the respective elements of $\mathbf{A}$ which reflect the relative importance of each criterion to the acquirer company. Thus the overall attraction of a target company could be summarized by the sum S

$$S = \mathbf{W} . \mathbf{A}$$

which could be used as an approximate means of ranking prospective target companies as indicated in Figure 5:4. Figures 5:3 and 5:4 remain somewhat conjectural in detail since the empirical part of the research into F-type acquirer company activity did not investigate the analytic techniques used in evaluating the gains from prospective target companies nor the methods, explicit or implicit, of ranking acquisition opportunities. These aspects would merit further research especially in the context of their relationship to capital budgeting concepts of discounted future cash flows.

Some implications for cash flow appraisal of target companies derive from the case study results noted in Figure 3:6 and from the emphasis placed by those interviewed upon the rapid realization of surplus assets and rationalization of remaining activities. The time scale over which the main changes were implemented appeared to be at most three years. Longer-term cash flows from remaining activities of the target company after rationalization and realization of surplus assets could be valued on a normal DCF basis. The early realization and rationalization phase is likely to be the most important component for valuation of the cash returns from acquisition partly because later cash flows are more heavily discounted (eg at a 20% discount rate the fourth year discount factor is 0.48) and partly because the early post-acquisition phase often includes the larger absolute cash flows – by way of property disposals, disposals of operating divisions, investment in retained divisions etc. Consequently long-term effects are probably of less importance in the appraisal of F-type acquisitions than in more general acquisitions of longer-term earnings streams where growth factors, stability of product and factor markets are all important variables in the DCF analysis. In fact the route to wealth creation by F-type acquisition activity is better described by a series of short-term opportunistic steps, rather as envisaged by Penrose (1966), each of which has a horizon of about three years, rather than by long-term project selection models. In the extreme case F-type activity could be regarded as maximizing liquidity growth per share; less readily realizable capital assets would have progressively less value as compared to cash.

Constraints, negotiation and offer package creation

The bid premium and negotiation model of Figure 4:3 is one component of a process which in practice is likely to be iterative. The target and acquirer company together define a financial state with regard to assets and earnings per share and loan stock covers which is a function of the financing instruments employed in the acquisition. Therefore negotiations that involve several possible bids and counter-bids, each of which determines a new financing solution, imply an iterative procedure that solves in a satisfactory manner the objectives of both the acquirer and target companies. Figures 5:5 and 5:6, together with Figure 4:3, describe the processes involved and their interactions with financial market constraints.

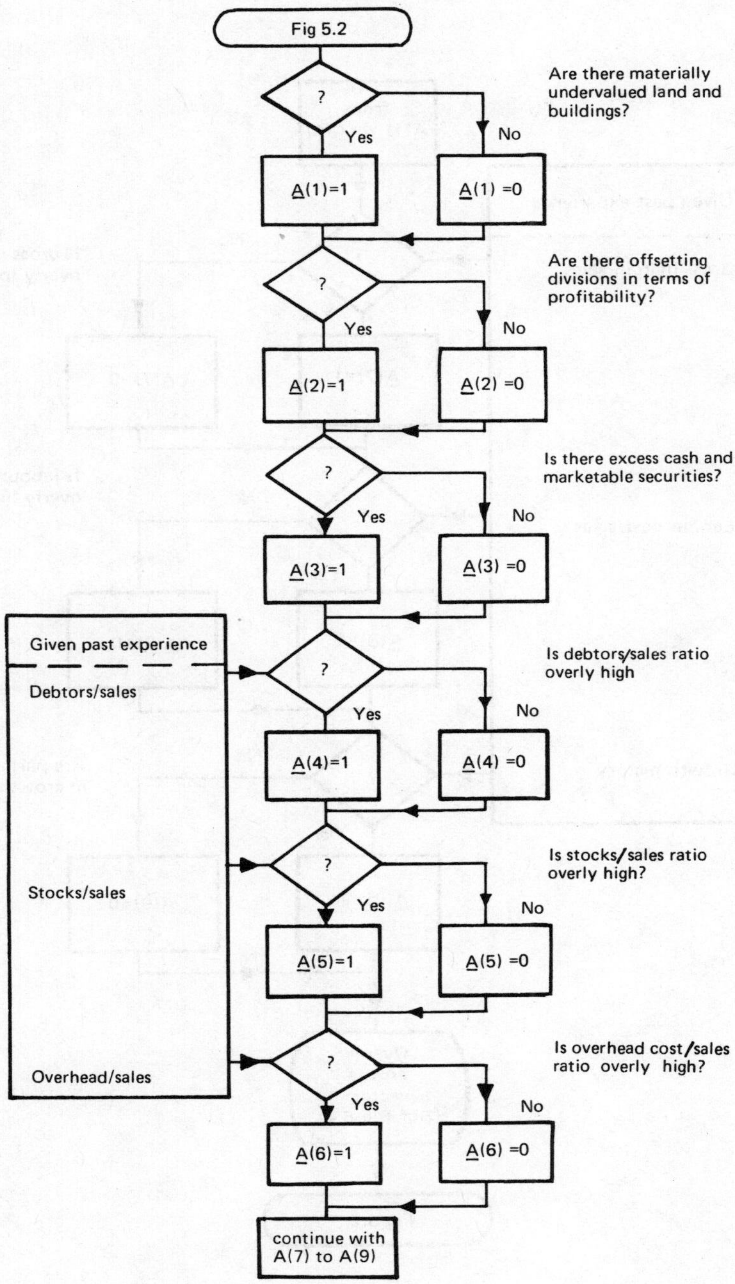

Figure 5:3 Prospect description routine

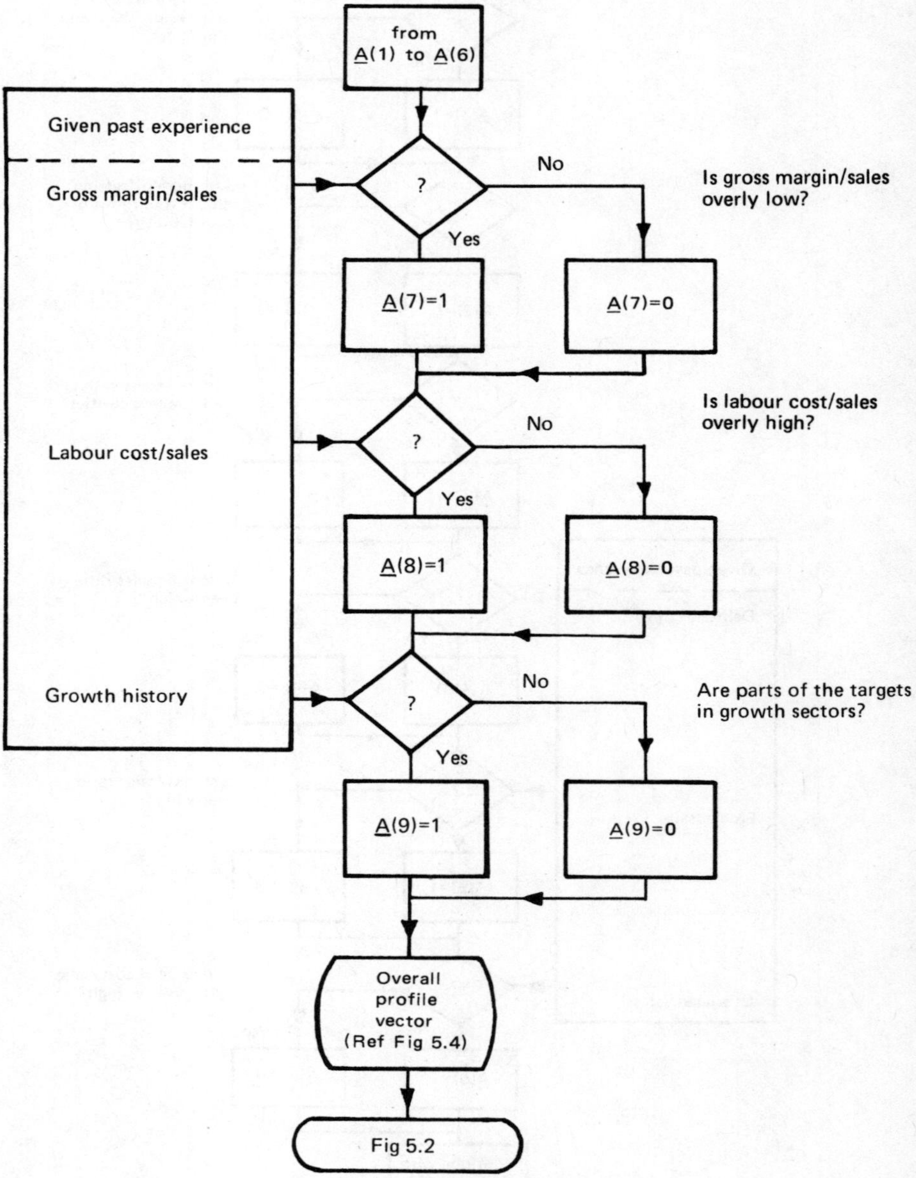

Figure 5:3 Prospect description routine (concluded)

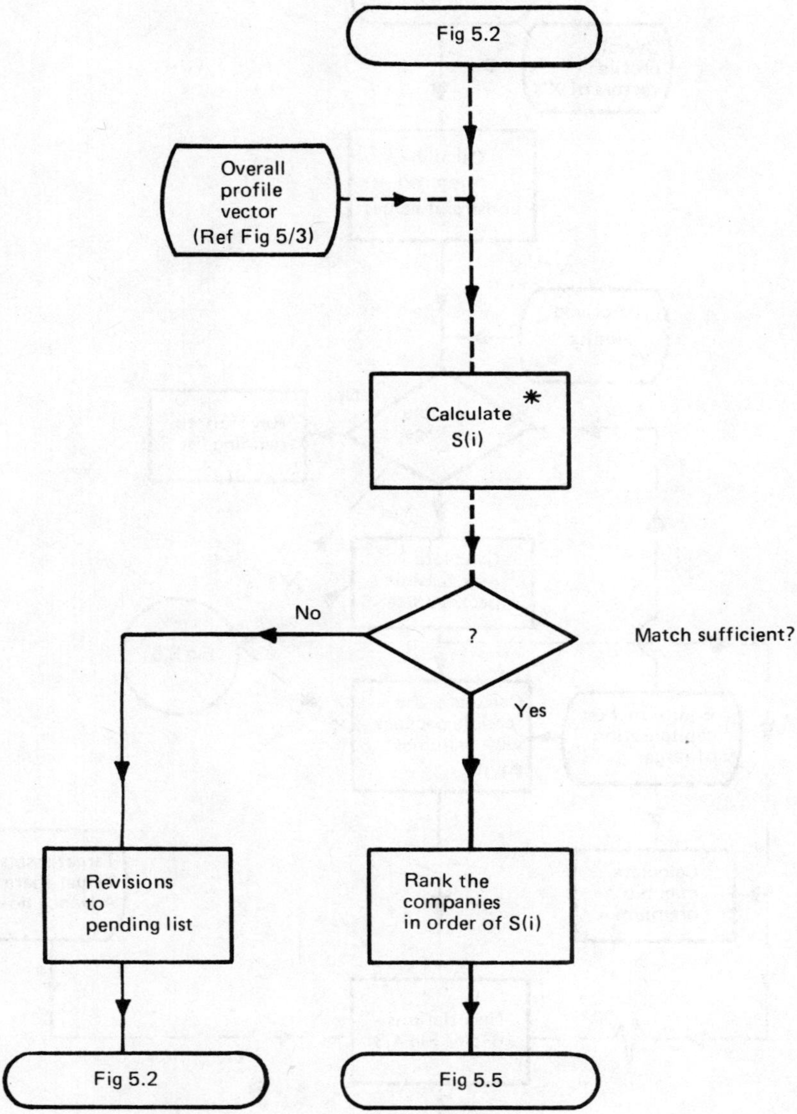

$$* \text{ Where } S(i) = \sum_{j=1}^{9} \underline{W}_A(j) \times \underline{A}(j)$$

Figure 5:4 Prospect evaluation routine

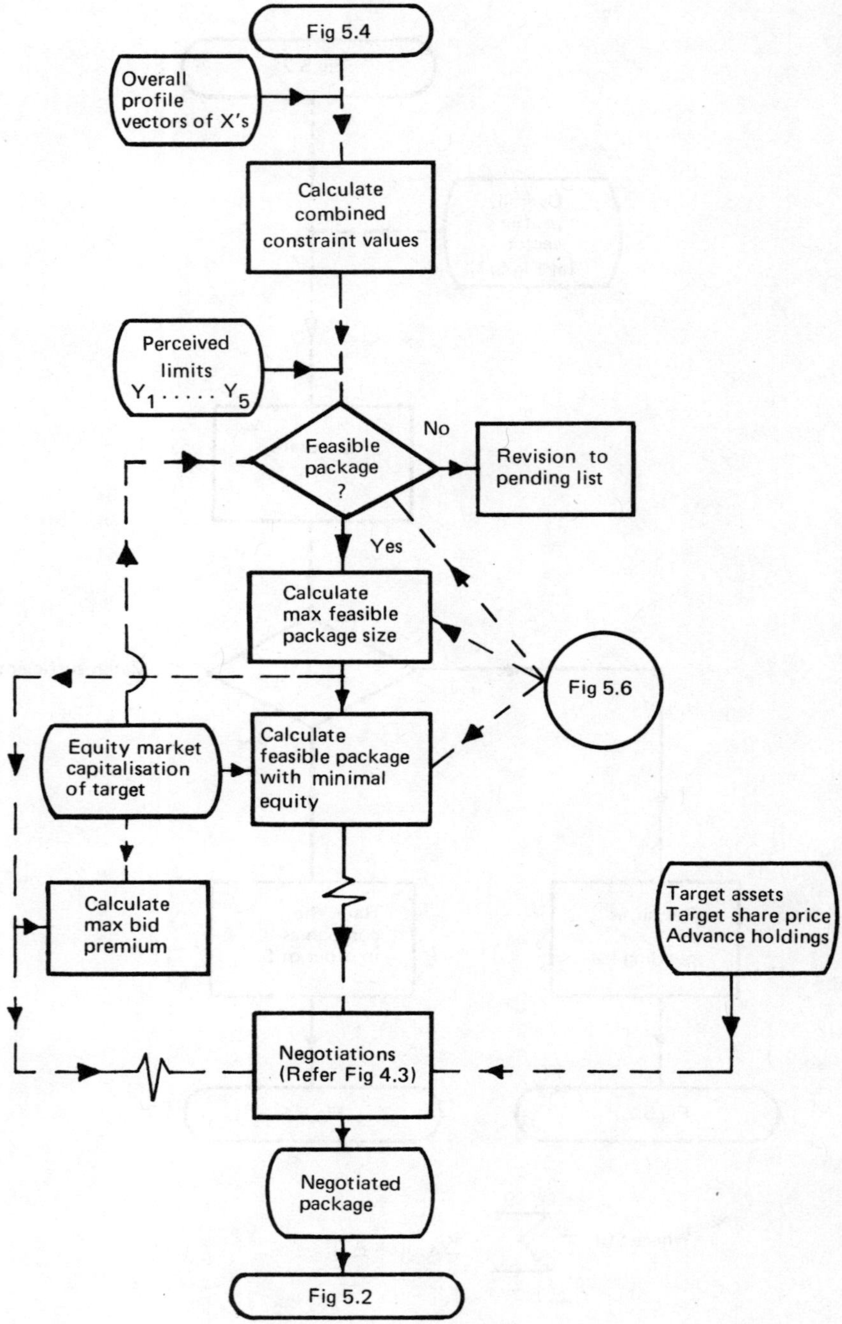

Figure 5:5 Constraints and offer package negotiations

Regarding Figure 5:5:

1 The Xs for acquirer and target company financial states yield the actual values of constraint measures from expressions C1 to C5 in Chapter 3. These are compared with the perceived constraint limits Y_1 to Y_5 to assess whether a feasible financial package exists. If not the prospective target is removed from a list of feasible acquisitions.

2 If a feasible financing package exists then negotiations can be commenced; perceived financial market constraints define a maximum acquisition size, ie exit capitalization for the target company. From the acquirer's viewpoint negotiations cannot exceed this figure without violation of constraints.

3 Negotiations can then be carried out with the target company and, as a result of negotiations, various financing methods examined until a suitable bargain is agreed which yields a negotiated package and incidentally a bid premium over the target company's pre-bid equity capitalization. Negotiations will be affected by the relative bargaining power of the acquirer and target companies. As discussed in Chapter 4, this will reflect advance holdings by the acquirer in the target company, the asset backing of the target company and the wishes of large block shareholders.

Regarding Figure 5:6:

1 Offer package creation is a step which may be carried out several times in the course of negotiations.

2 As discussed in Chapter 4 under 'negotiation issues' the bargaining process may be affected if there are any large blocks of shareholders in the target company. These blocks can work for or against the acquirer's interest depending upon whether the block shareholders aim to encourage counter-bids or are happy to have the opportunity to sell out *in toto*. However the acquirer will almost certainly need to negotiate with major shareholders even if they are not directors of the target company.

3 The acquirer would want to finance the acquisition at minimum cost. This implies using cash and then loan stocks up to the maximum constrained levels prior to issuing equity.

4 Changes in interest rates and equity markets during the period of a bid or negotiations will affect the attractions of the financing package and may necessitate revisions.

5 Programming techniques such as linear programming could be employed to minimize the cost of the financing package provided linear approximations are in order. (The constraint equations outlined in Chapter 3 are not linear in the Xs and Ys unless δX_6^A is zero and the interest rates are assumed constant for changes in loan content of the offer package.) Otherwise non-linear or heuristic methods are required.

6 For a given set of constraint levels (which might in practice be obtained from discussion with institutional investors, merchant bankers, stockbrokers

etc) the constraint equations outlined in Chapter 3 could be rearranged to yield the Xs in terms of the Ys since the offer package creation is a problem in solving the Xs .

Summary

The growth process of companies involved in growth by acquisition is one of sudden changes in financial structure and capital assets. Consequently search and evaluation procedures must be adaptive to incorporate past changes in the basis for analysis of subsequent acquisition proposals.

The number of potential acquisitions can be considerably reduced by the adoption of search processes and criteria which incorporate constraints on feasible acquisitions. Although the foregoing discussion is primarily concerned with financial matters, constraints by way of industry, geographical area of operations, product lines etc could be incorporated in the same framework.

The external contacts of a firm are likely to play an important part in producing proposals for acquisition. For financial matters and financially-oriented growth, 'city' institutions and financial advisers are likely to be important sources of proposals.

Objective description and evaluation of acquisition proposals can be assembled into a form for ranking possible target companies according to criteria consistent with overall acquisition objectives.

Acquisition bargaining procedures and the creation of a financing package are integrated procedures. Creation of a financing package should reflect financial market constraints. The bid premium is a consequence of the financing package. As a general rule acquirer companies should seek to use cash and loan stock prior to equity for acquisition financing.

Continuing files should be kept on potential target companies. The attraction of any particular target company is likely to vary with financial market conditions and the relative performance of acquirer and target companies.

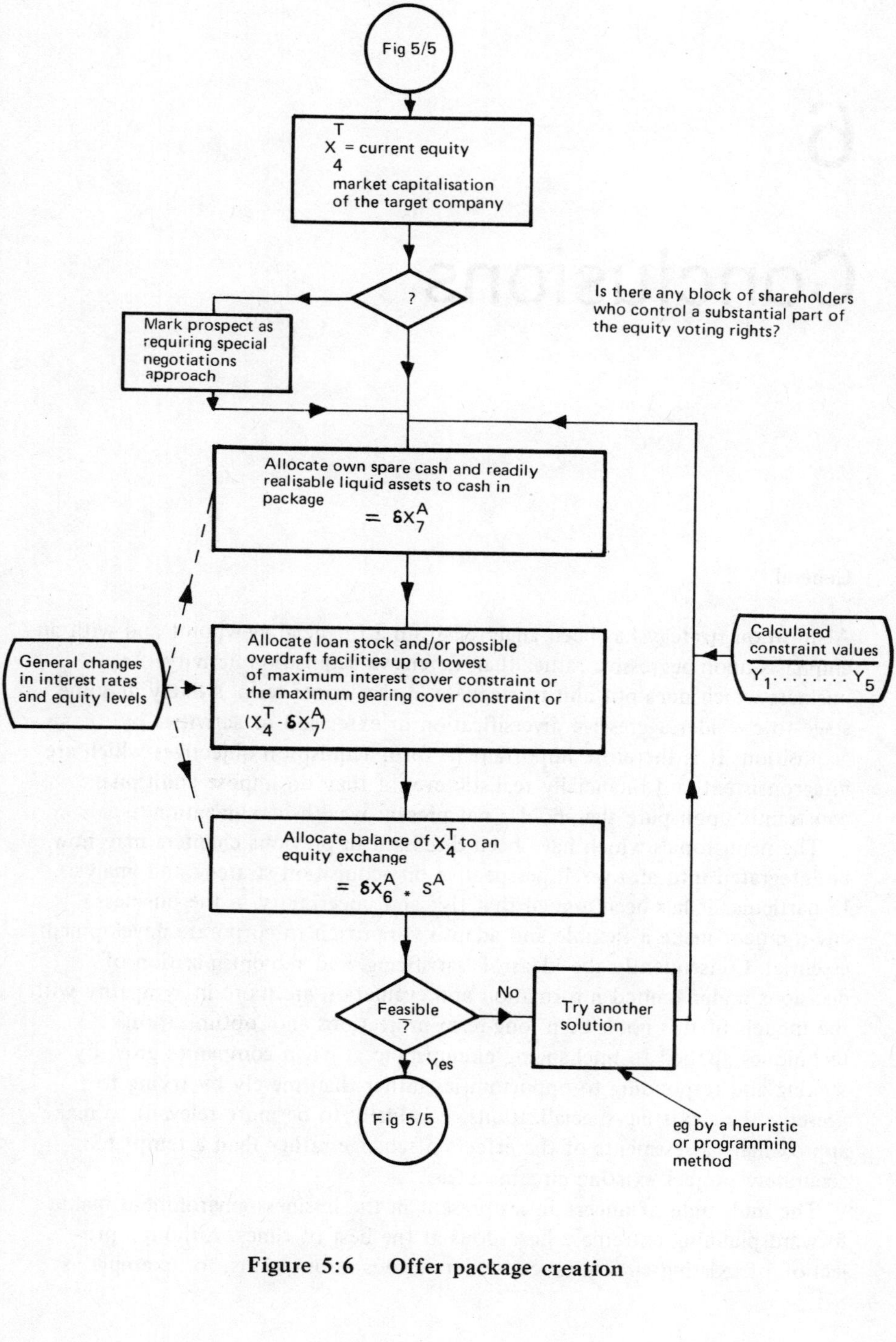

Figure 5:6 Offer package creation

6

Conclusions

General

Acquisition strategy has been analysed from a financial viewpoint and with an emphasis upon aggressive rather than defensive acquisition activity. Any business which does not aim to stagnate in the longer term is likely at some stage to consider aggressive diversification or extension of activities by acquisition. It is therefore important to form acquisition objectives which are interconsistent and financially realistic even if they do impose additional constraints upon pure shareholder net present wealth maximization.

The main topics which have been discussed in previous chapters may now be integrated into an overall perspective on acquisition strategy and analysis. In particular it has been argued that risk and uncertainty in the business environment make a flexible and adaptive approach to corporate development essential. Consequently the ideas of 'satisficing' and sub-optimization of decisions under limited information and evaluation are more in sympathy with the models of this book than long-term projections and 'optimization' techniques applied to unchanging circumstances. When companies grow by seeking and responding to opportunities rather than merely by trying to preserve their existing specializations, it is likely to be more relevant to make approximate assessments of the effects of change rather than attempt to accurately project existing circumstances.

The multitude of uncertainties present in the business environment makes forward planning extremely hazardous at the best of times. Although projection of existing circumstances under various assumptions, for example as to real growth rates, inflation rates, taxes and cost structures, will almost certainly differ from the final outcome, such analysis can be most valuable in exposing problem areas and the need for change. Therefore strategy for corporate development, of which acquisition strategy is an important component, can benefit from the use of models, first to project existing circumstances and second to allow appraisal of proposals for structural change by way of capital investment projects. Examples of the former class of models have been outlined in Lawson and Bean (1975) whereas this discussion of acquisition strategy is an example of the latter type of model.

The timing of acquisitions is of critical importance. Whereas the performance of public companies can best be appraised, from a shareholder's viewpoint, by reference to equity movements relative to an index of share prices, the private company does not have the same reference point. Financing of acquisitions involving public companies is dependent upon the state of the stock market so far as equity valuation and selection of financing instruments are concerned. Acquisitive private companies are likely to make their best acquisitions when business confidence and Stock Exchange prices are at a low ebb since cash is a readily accepted medium for financing deals and the cash value of assets at such times is near a minimum due to tight monetary circumstances.

The aspiring acquisitor is likely to find mental if not physical models useful both on a macro- and a micro-level. The former can help in indicating timing and financial package content of acquisition deals and the latter can clarify the search and evaluation methods for specific target companies as well as serving, by cash flow projection models, to give early warning of potential difficulties from existing operations.

Specific concepts in acquisition strategy and appraisal

The shareholder net present wealth maximization viewpoint was adopted for development of the models of acquisition strategy on the grounds that executives in financially-oriented acquirer companies tended to hold substantial equity interests in their companies. However, as more and more social considerations enter into the business environment largely as a result of governmental statutory interference, this objective becomes complicated by considerations of employment, environmental protection, taxation, excessive union power etc. Most of these additional factors can be seen as cost constraints leaving a residual wealth available to shareholders. At the corporate level it has been argued that the marginal cash flows available to the acquirer company shareholders are the relevant data for capital investment analysis. For publicly quoted acquirer companies the wealth-inducing effects for shareholders are exhibited in stock market price movements. Given that shareholders generally hold several securities, acquisitions should aim to enhance portfolio risk-and-return characteristics.

So long as shareholders have a spread of investments, the assessment of risk-return characteristics of the target and acquirer companies jointly and together can follow from the estimation of systematic risk relative to the so-called 'market portfolio' for which a suitable index of security prices, eg the Financial Times All-Share Index, can provide a reasonable approximation. Only if one of the combining parties has a negative systematic risk with respect to the market will there be any likelihood that increased expected returns by way of cash flows can reduce shareholder wealth through excessive increase in risk. Ideally a prospective acquisition should both increase return and decrease risk, both measures being related to share price movements rather than corporate cash flows.

The emphasis upon share price movements starts from the viewpoint that share prices do not contain any 'intrinsic worth' but are simply a supply/demand market in their own right. It was for this reason that share price movements were discussed in some detail and their random nature noted. Characterization of price movements in statistical terms is important for the quantification of risk relevant to portfolio theory and the interaction of risk and discount rates. If price movements are best approximated by the stable Paretian model then portfolio diversification is less valuable as the distribution characteristic exponent (a) decreases from 2.0 towards 1.0. A further consequence of decreasing a is the increased probability of large price changes associated with the tails of distribution of share price movements. Increasing probability of large price changes correspondingly enhances the value of deferred equity rights such as those associated with warrants and convertibles.

Constrained acquisition search and evaluation

The previous chapter developed a model of the acquisition search and evaluation processes, which contained static and dynamic aspects. The former was concerned with analysis of potential acquisition opportunities at particular points in time and the latter was concerned with incorporating changes internal and external to the firm to provide an updated basis for evaluating new acquisition proposals. Since relative company circumstances and profitability alter with time, possible target companies which may be unattractive acquisition candidates at one point may at a subsequent time prove attractive. Regular monitoring of possible target companies is an important aspect of acquisition analysis.

The objective of increasing shareholder net present wealth together with the impact of financial market constraints considerably restricts the range of potential target companies. Efficient search procedures have featured prominently in the development of behavioural theories of the firm; works by Simon (1955) and Clarkson (1962) are indicative of the need to reduce the variety of choice available to decision-makers to manageable proportions. Indeed it is important to organize search procedures in such a way that only relevant acquisition proposals are received, otherwise costs of search and of detailed evaluation can quickly escalate. Of the financial market constraints, maximum size and either assets or earnings per share in relation to the acquirer company can be used for rapid screening-out of unsuitable acquisitions. Minimum acquisition size with respect to expenditure of effort post-acquisition may be a further criterion which can be used to screen out irrelevant prospects. Additional non-financial criteria which have only briefly been mentioned might include industry, geographical location, stage in the production/distribution cycle etc. Figure 5:3 may be amended as necessary to include different or additional criteria for particular acquisition strategies.

The use of internal and external contacts of the firm as mechanisms for generating acquisition proposals can also play an important role in producing relevant acquisition proposals. Internal managers and employees of a firm, particularly sales and marketing personnel, frequently have knowledge about the performance of competitors or of closely related products which may disclose acquisition opportunities. Production personnel may have suggestions as to vertical or horizontal integration moves for gaining access respectively to special sources of supply or additional capacity. Financial managers should be encouraged to develop banking and 'city' contacts with stockbrokers, merchant bankers etc in order to promote a flow of acquisition ideas from external sources.

Capital appraisal of acquisition proposals

Adoption of a portfolio viewpoint to corporate investment decision-making to the end that capital investments are only undertaken if they benefit shareholder portfolios implies revision of the more usual discounted cash flow model as a company specific method of capital appraisal and the introduction of a general shareholder approach. Until the link between changes in expected corporate cash flows and share price movements is formally investigated, it is not clear what model should be used under conditions of business risk. This area is one in which further research could be conducted at both a practical and a theoretical level.

The focus of appraisal with reference to portfolio shareholders bypasses accepted cost of capital reference points for capital budget analysis. If the systematic risk analysis of target and acquirer companies indicates that increased return and/or reduced risk will result from the acquisition and if the deal satisfies financial market constraints in the short term then there is a prima facie case for deciding in favour of the acquisition. Cash flow projection is largely a supporting analysis to assessment of portfolio advantage. Marginal cash flows should have a favourable risk-return profile for the acquirer company's shareholders; the method of assessment could follow the outline in Chapter 2. In cases where returns do not come about for some time then financial market constraints will not be met and the acquisition will prove hard to justify to shareholders. Although this approach is possibly more stringent than normal discounted cash flow analysis of capital projects, due to the emphasis on short-term performance, it may be more realistic in that effectively the larger the deal relative to the acquirer company the more important it becomes to avoid short-term dilution in shareholders' wealth. One may argue that a payback approach to capital investment analysis whereby projects are ranked preferentially in order of payback period for a given discount rate is a suitable ('satisficing') rule for stressing the short-term advantages or disadvantages of investment projects which have considerable uncertainty; a discussion of discounted cash flow and payback methods of capital appraisal is amplified in a paper by Haynes and Solomon (1962).

The financial market constraints fit quite naturally into programming models of corporate financing. Although non-linear as specified, assumption of constant interest rates with respect to amounts borrowed, and an absence of equity content in an acquisition-financing package, would result in linear constraints and therefore possible inclusion in linear-programming corporate models. One such model is that of Carleton (1969) which focuses on maximizing the net present value of dividend flows to shareholders. Carleton conceives of a 'macro'-model which handles the consumption/investment choice of shareholders, transmission of cash between time periods and raising of funds and cash flows relating to a set of investment projects. Within the macro-model lies a 'micro'-model which handles the capital investment projects of the firm. However Carleton's model would not necessarily be consistent with a portfolio viewpoint for Lintner's reasons as outlined in Chapter 2. For readers who wish to build upon Carleton's ideas and incorporate the financial market constraints, Carleton's capital budget M_t is the externally constrained source of funds and corresponds to the financial market incentives through constraint C6 of Chapter 3, rearranged to yield

$$M_t = X_4^T - \delta X_7^A = \delta X_2^A + \delta X_6^A * S^A$$

Programming methods have also been proposed as a means of corporate planning with constraints on reported results such as return on assets, profits in successive years etc – see Chambers (1967).

Acquisition bargaining and creation of financing packages

The bargaining between acquirer and target company is the process by which the acquirer incidentally solves his financing-cum-investment decision. It is therefore important for the acquirer to realize exactly within what limits he can bargain yet retain a viable acquisition. The financial limits are set by the prior financial states of the acquirer and target companies, namely assets and earnings per share, equity capitalizations, loan stock interest and principal covers.

However, as discussed in Chapter 4, the acquirer company can expect a somewhat different bargaining approach from the target company if it is controlled by a few large shareholders who cannot readily sell out on the open market. In addition the bargaining process can be viewed as a game where, as

Stapleton (1971) has pointed out, it can pay both parties to influence the expectations of the other depending upon the acquisition-financing package.

The bargaining process is likely to be iterative in practice, perhaps along the lines of Figures 5:5 and 5:6. Counter-bidders are more likely to appear in circumstances where large block-holders exist in the target company, if only because such holders may quite logically be prepared to accept a lower exit value than other smaller shareholders.

The acquirer company can enhance its bargaining hand by market operations, although tightening of the City Code and prospective companies' legislation may well detract from the possibilities which were available at the time of the underlying research for this book. Nevertheless potential acquirers should make as much use as possible of market operations since they tend to lower the necessary exit price and financing costs. Bid defences on the other hand should aim to prevent market operations, stress the value of asset backing and generally overestimate future profitability. Bid premiums have been described as a consequence of other activity and are likely to reflect asset backing of the target company, the amount of equity involved in the financing package and the bargaining strength of the acquirer company.

Valuation of financing instruments is complex once deferred equity rights are introduced. Convertibles and warrants can be valuable if the expected volatility of share prices is high in relation to discount effects. The acquirer would normally want to defer exercise of equity rights and arrange exercise terms or share performance to preclude future equity dilution.

Appendices

1

Conditions for increased portfolio value through acquisition

Analysis of the effects of an acquisition upon various investor portfolios may be carried out using the mean-variance portfolio selection model developed by Markowitz, Sharpe and Lintner. There are three sets of circumstances which require examination, namely:

1 The effect upon portfolio investors who hold the acquirer company securities in their portfolios.
2 The effect upon portfolio investors who hold the target company securities in their portfolios.
3 The effect upon portfolio investors who hold both target and acquirer company securities in their portfolios.

The three cases can be examined by a common model with slightly different interpretations respectively. It is assumed that investors are risk-averse and aim to maximize a utility function which may be expressed in mean-variance terms.

Let $\overline{U}(\overline{R}_p, \sigma_p)$ be the utility function relating to a portfolio of securities which investors wish to maximize. Denote quantities of a stock or portfolio of stocks held by X_{pj} where p refers to the portfolio and j to individual stocks or a combination of stocks in the portfolio.

Prior to an acquisition the investor holds only a quantity X_{pj} of securities j affected by the acquisition as a component of his portfolio. The change in portfolio utility for a change in the expected return $\overline{R}$ and a change in variance of securities j are respectively:

$$\frac{\partial \bar{U}}{\partial \bar{R}_j} = \frac{\partial \bar{U}}{\partial \bar{R}_p} \cdot \frac{\partial \bar{R}_p}{\partial \bar{R}_j} = X_{pj} \cdot \frac{\partial \bar{U}}{\partial \bar{R}_p} > 0 \text{ if } X_{pj} > 0$$

$$\frac{\partial \bar{U}}{\partial \sigma_j} = \frac{\partial \bar{U}}{\partial \sigma_p} \cdot \frac{\partial \sigma_p}{\partial \sigma_j}$$

If only long positions are held so that $X_{pj} > 0$ then any increase in $\bar{R}_j$ will increase the overall $\bar{U}(\bar{R}_p, \sigma_p)$. Provided that $\bar{R}_j$ is not decreased by an acquisition then the relevant criterion of increasing shareholder wealth will be that the change in overall portfolio utility for a change in variance in security j is increased, assuming that investors are risk-averse so that $\partial \bar{U}/\partial \sigma_p < 0$. This criterion will be satisfied if $\partial \sigma_p / \partial \sigma_j < 0$.

The cases that are to be investigated may be studied within the case of an overall portfolio p containing a number of stocks in two subsidiary portfolios X_A and X_B. For this case, denoting the correlation coefficient between returns on X_A and X_B by r_{AB},

$$\sigma_p^2 = X_A^2 \sigma_A^2 + 2X_A X_B r_{AB} \sigma_A \sigma_B + X_B^2 \sigma_B^2$$

$$\frac{\partial \sigma_p}{\partial \sigma_B} = \frac{X_B(X_A r_{AB} \sigma_A + X_B \sigma_B)}{\sigma_p}$$

and

$$\frac{\partial \sigma_p}{\partial \sigma_B} < 0 \quad \text{only if, for long holdings of A and B,}$$

$$X_A r_{AB} \sigma_A + X_B \sigma_B < 0$$

or

$$r_{AB} < -\frac{X_B}{X_A} \cdot \frac{\sigma_B}{\sigma_A}$$

This condition requires that r_{AB} be negative and, depending upon the values of X_A, X_B, σ_B, σ_A, less than one.

Case 1

In this case portfolio A should be interpreted as the investor's portfolio excluding the investment in the acquirer shares which comprise investment B. Only in cases where the correlation between B and the remainder of the portfolio is negative as a result of the acquisition will there be problems in assessing whether an increase in $\bar{R}_B$ and/or a decrease in σ_B is beneficial to investors.

Case 2

Here investors are presented with a switch of holding from target company securities to securities in a revised earnings stream based upon target plus acquirer cash flows. From the acquirer's viewpoint it is necessary to assess whether the target securities X_B are correlated positively or negatively with the portfolios held by target company shareholders. In the absence of special circumstances the market portfolio would be a sensible reference for comparative purposes. (Large shareholders in the target could be consulted to establish whether their overall portfolios have special characteristics.) Again the point is to establish whether the switch of securities, allowing for changes in the future cash flows as a result of the acquisition, alters the correlation sign between existing target returns to shareholders and the returns of the combined companies to the target shareholders. If not then one may presume that increases in $\overline{R}_B$ and/or decreases in σ_B are desirable.

Case 3

In this case X_B represents a portfolio of securities in both the target and acquirer company securities. The problem is to assess whether the modifications to the combined returns to shareholders benefit overall portfolio holders. It will only be in doubt, assuming that $\overline{R}_B$ increases and/or σ_B decreases as a result of the acquisition, if the correlation of returns between the remainder of the portfolio A and the combined portfolio B of target and acquirer is negative. In fact Cases 1 and 2 may be seen as special cases of Case 3 where holdings pre-acquisition in either the acquirer or target company are zero.

Summary

Provided some increment is achieved in the expected returns of the combining companies or some decrease in the variance of those returns is achieved then the acquisition is likely to be beneficial to portfolio holders. Only where the combining companies include one set of returns which are negatively correlated either with the portfolios of existing investors or with each other could this proviso not apply. In such a case the relative values of the holdings and the correlation of their returns before and after the acquisition need to be considered in greater depth.

2

Companies classified as financially oriented acquirer companies over the period October 1965–March 1972 inclusive

Adepton
Argo Caribbean
Argyle Securities
Armour Trust
Bank Bridge Securities
Barclay Securities
Cannon Street Investments
Direct Spanish Telegraph
Dowgate & General Investments
Drakes
Dundee Perth & London Securities
Eastern & General Holdings
Eastern Produce (Holdings)
Eldridge Stableford
First National Finance Corporation
First National Industrial Trust
Grimshawe-Windsor
Hanson Trust
Heenan Beddow
Hestair
Jessel Securities
King's Motors (Oxford)
Kniton Investments
Leeds Assets
Lewston Developments
Lex-Service Group
Ralli International
Rothschild Investment Trust
Slater Walker Securities
Spey Investments
Sterling Guarantee Trust
Tower Assets
Tremletts
Vavasseur (J.H.)

In addition the following companies were classified as property-oriented acquirer companies, ie those growing by acquisition but with the main emphasis upon property investment.

Amalgamated Investment & Property
Cornwall Property (Holdings)
Galliford Estates

3

Calculation of financial constraints

The example concerns two companies both of which are suppliers to the textile industry. There would have been considerable commercial logic for a merger or acquisition between them since both had excess plant capacity and valuable freehold sites. The balance sheets indicate the lack of borrowings and excess liquidity, especially in company B. At the time of analysis the companies had respective ordinary share capitalizations of:

	Company A	*Company B*
Share price	16¾p	22½p
Ordinary shares in issue	4 982 128	3 973 744
Capitalization	£0.84 million	£0.89 million

Accounting information for corresponding periods is given for both companies. It is likely that realizable values for the freehold properties of both companies exceed book values especially in the case of company B, but in the absence of more detailed information book values will be used for illustrative purposes. Calculation of the values of the Xs (see Chapter 3, under 'Formalization of objectives') are shown subsequent to the accounts. Since either company might consider acquisition of the other as their sizes are approximately the same, the distinction of one as acquirer and one as target remains to be discussed.

Profit and Loss Accounts in £s

	Company A	*Company B*
Sales	3 874 000	2 228 000
Profits pre-interest	235 437	174 129
Interest	38 870	890
Profits pre-tax	196 567	173 239
Taxation	117 780	78 866
Profits after tax	78 787	94 373
Preference dividend	13 925	14 625
Earnings on ordinary shares	64 862	79 748
Ordinary dividend	37 366	61 701
Retained earnings	27 496	18 047

Balance Sheet in £s

			Company A
FIXED ASSETS	Cost	Depreciation	Net
Freehold and long leasehold land and buildings*	672 578	222 394	450 184
Short leaseholds	13 423	1 752	11 671
Plant and machinery	2 289 990	1 467 190	822 800
	2 975 991	1 691 336	1 284 655
Trade investments			500
			1 285 155
CURRENT ASSETS			
Stocks			1 358 766
Debtors and prepayments			924 347
Cash and deposits			–
			2 283 113
less			
CURRENT LIABILITIES			
Creditors and accruals			438 002
Taxation payable			76 494
Dividends payable			37 366
Bank overdrafts			409 014
			960 876
Net current assets			1 322 237
Total net assets			2 607 392
Represented by:			
DEFERRED LIABILITIES			
Taxation			20 000
Loans			–
			20 000
ISSUED SHARE CAPITAL AND RESERVES			
Cumulative preference shares of £1 each**			174 060
Ordinary shares of 25p each			1 245 532
Capital reserves			187 985
Revenue reserves			979 815
			2 587 392
Total long-term liabilities			2 607 392

Notes

* The directors considered that freehold land and buildings had a higher market value than that shown in the balance sheet but that the difference is not material in relation to trading activities.

** The preference shares carry an 8% coupon.

Balance Sheet in £s

			Company B
FIXED ASSETS	**Cost**	**Depreciation**	**Net**
Freehold land and buildings*	558 066	106 846	451 220
Plant and machinery	1 241 561	798 403	443 158
	1 799 627	905 249	894 378
Goodwill arising on consolidation			153 682
Trade investments (Directors' valuation £159 000)			117 524
			1 165 584
CURRENT ASSETS			
Stocks			694 655
Debtors and prepayments			621 577
Cash and deposits			107 876
			1 424 108
less			
CURRENT LIABILITIES			
Creditors and accruals			255 139
Taxation payable			45 446
Dividends payable			41 832
			342 417
Net current assets			1 081 691
Total net assets			2 247 275
Represented by:			
DEFERRED LIABILITIES			
Taxation			73 000
Loans			11 132
			84 132
ISSUED SHARE CAPITAL AND RESERVES			
Cumulative preference shares of £1 each**			195 000
Ordinary shares of 25p each			993 436
Capital reserves			78 869
Revenue reserves			895 838
			2 163 143
Total long-term liabilities			2 247 275

Notes

* The directors consider that a revaluation of land and buildings (on a going-concern basis) would exceed book value but the excess would not be material to group operations.

** The preference shares carry a coupon of 7½%.

Calculation of Constraint Xs

Values in £s

	Company A	*Company B*
X_1	235 437	174 129
X_2	409 014	11 132
X_3	2 433 332 (note 1)	1 887 461 (note 2)
X_4	840 000	890 000
X_5	64 862	79 748
X_6	4 982 128	3 973 744
δX_7	–	74 000 (note 3)
I	9.5% (note 4)	8.0% (note 5)
S (note 6)	16¾p	22½p

Notes

1 Calculated as £2 607 392 less preference shares of £174 060

2 Calculated as:

total net assets			£2 247 275
less	goodwill	£153 682	
	preference	195 000	
	loans	11 132	359 814
			£1 887 461

3 Calculated as £107 876 less £33 876 (which is approximately 1½% of turnover) in order to leave some cash to finance transactions

4 Calculated as £38 870 x 100.0/ £409 014

5 Calculated as £890 x 100.0/ £11 132

6 100p = £1

Examination of the constraints C1 – C4 as defined in Chapter 3, under 'Formalization of objectives' shows that in terms of relative size the capitalizations are approximately equal. Existence of a bid premium would almost certainly imply breach of the acquisition-size constraint. However it will be clear from the subsequent discussion that breach of this constraint by up to (say) 20% will not detract from compliance with the other constraints.

Loan stock covers

Constraint C2 concerning profits cover shows that there is a debt capacity of up to £2 060 000 on the present profits of the combined companies given an interest cover of 2, or £783 000 of loan stock given a conservative cover of four times out of pre-tax pre-interest profits and assuming SI^A at 8% per annum.

Constraint 3 concerning net tangible assets cover shows that there is a debt capacity of £3 826 647 given an equal debt:equity ratio or £1 703 250 with a more conservative limit of 50% debt:equity. Therefore debt interest cover is much tighter constraint than net tangibles in this case.

Dilution constraints

Assuming that one company acquired the other with £1 200 000 of 8% loan stock, giving a premium of over 35%, it is necessary to calculate the dilution implications. Using constraints C3 and C4 it is clear that no dilution in assets or earnings per share would arise (8% was the going rate on a convertible loan at the time of the accounts for the companies concerned).

Overall comments

Either company could acquire the other by a loan stock financed acquisition. A convertible loan would have to fit in with dilution considerations by way of C3 and C4 but adequate leeway exists whichever company is the acquirer. Company B has the advantage of £74 000 of free cash and a higher capitalization but Company A has higher profits and assets. Company B had a somewhat more volatile profit performance than Company A in the years preceding that for which results are shown.

4

Acquisition questionnaire

This questionnaire indicates some of the detailed information which an acquirer company would generally want to obtain as part of its procedures for acquisition appraisal of a target company.

1 Statutory information

Company Name
- Address
- Registered office
- Location of statutory books
- Authorized capital
- Issued capital
- Memorandum
- Articles

2 Directors and secretary

- Name
- Address
- Responsibilities
- Age
- Qualifications
- Previous job history
- Other interests
- Salary
- Pension rights
- Years of contract outstanding
- Fringe benefits
- Shareholding and options

3 Register of shareholders

- Shareholders controlling over 2% of the issued capital
- Institutional shareholders
  - Number
  - Average holding
  - Average duration of holding

Private shareholders
- Number
- Average holding
- Average duration of holding

4 Subsidiary and associated companies
- Name
- Location of business
- Details of business
- % of capital held
- Other interests

For each material company controlled by the potential target company, the following information should be obtained.

1 Employees
- Number by category and average salary
  - Directorate
  - Central administration
  - Production
  - Marketing and sales
  - Other
- Details of pension schemes, share incentive schemes
  - Employees with contracts of employment in excess of one year
  - Training schemes, training board aid
  - Professionally qualified staff and respective ages
  - Overtime schemes
  - Holiday arrangements
  - Special incentives

2 Sales and markets
- Description of product range and age of products
- Geographical spread of markets
- Methods of distribution employed
- Agency and factor agreements
- Export percentages
- Gross margins on product range by home and export sales
- History of home and export sales levels
- Number of customers
- Advertising policies pursued, special promotions
- Sales literature
- Annual changes in prices of major products over the last five years
- Details of new technologies or innovations over the last five years and of their commercial success

3 Production and supply
- Location of production facilities
- Employees per unit of production
- Main inputs to production process
- Major suppliers
- Details and duration of major supply contracts
- Prices of major inputs to production over the last three years
- Strike records by production location
- Number of skilled and unskilled workers
- Duration of production process
- Vulnerability to world commodity market price changes

4 Financial
- Land and buildings
  - Location, plans, age and condition
  - Utilization
  - Expansion possibilities
  - Date and cost of original purchase
  - Balance sheet value
  - Estimated market value
  - Most recent valuation and valuers
  - Freehold/leasehold details
  - Mortgages or charges on the property
  - Tenancies
  - Planning restrictions
- Patents, trade marks, licences – agreements and revenues
- Plant and machinery, motor vehicles
  - Major items
  - Utilization
  - Lease or hire-purchase agreements outstanding
  - Basis of depreciation
  - Book and tax written-down values
  - Average age
- Investments
  - Details of long-term trade investments and loans
  - Market and cost values of quoted securities
- Stocks
  - Methods of valuation
  - Period of obsolescence
  - Seasonal factors
  - Classification as between raw materials, work in progress, finished goods
  - Value added % to input materials
  - Output per employee
  - Stock records

Receivables
- Listing of aged receivables
- List of bad debts
- Special discounts offered
- Factor agreements
- Seasonal factors
- Special credit arrangements with customers

Bank balances
- Overdraft limits
- Security requirements
- Bankers and length of relationship

Payables
- Listing of aged payables
- Details of special credit arrangements

Loans
- Amounts, interest rates, repayment details, securities given

General
- Balance sheet
- Five years' historical results with sales and costs of sales
- Point to which tax liabilities are agreed, settled
- Insurance policies and covers
- Accounting staff and regularity of reports
- Details of management accounting reports

5 Economic and political influences
- Cyclical nature of earnings, cash flows
- Share price movements relative to stock market indices
- Level of gearing
- Product diversification or specialization
- Insulation from national economic fluctuations
- Insulation from political interference
- Dependence on government contracts or special customers
- Consumer or industrial product markets
- Requirements for transactions financing
- Growth of product market sectors
- Vulnerability to price controls
- Vulnerability to trade union power

5

Research methods and procedure

The existing literature surrounding mergers and acquisitions, both the academic and the more managerially-oriented literature, tends to generalize across the range of acquisition practice. However acquisitions may be motivated by many factors acting singly or in combination such as product market protection, economies of scale, extending executive power and fiscal advantage. This research specifically focused upon 'financially-oriented' acquisitions which in the UK have tended to carry the lable 'asset-stripping' and which might be thought of as a somewhat more financially sophisticated extension of the earlier US conglomerate era. The aim of the research was to build models to explain the acquisition aims and procedures of financially-oriented acquirer companies.

The models were principally descriptive and attempted to show how financial strategy in acquisition decisions was affected by the environmental context within which the companies operated. Therefore the models contained parts which were relatively better tested than others with respect to the empirical data; some parts of the model contained functional mathematical specifications whereas others contained qualitative relationships. Although the models may be considered to offer prescriptive messages for financial executives they were not designed to provide predictive mechanisms for future financial behaviour since the political and economic environment in the UK is in a state of rapid change with respect to acquisition practices and financial market activities.

The research primarily adopted a financial basis for explanation; in particular it took capital budgeting and portfolio theories as reference points. This is not to deny that the subject matter might have been approached from other view-points, eg from organizational theory or as a study in the psychology of top executives, but rather that business finance was considered *a priori* to offer the most suitable explanatory basis. It also reflected the author's interests, prior training and business contacts.

Research population of companies

In the context of UK companies shown illustratively below the research focused on subset D which itself was a hypothesized group of firms. The models were created with population D in view and the generalizations of the research were not intended to extend beyond population D. Nevertheless the extent of D as a component of acquisition activity illustrated by area C was an empirical fact to be established by the research.

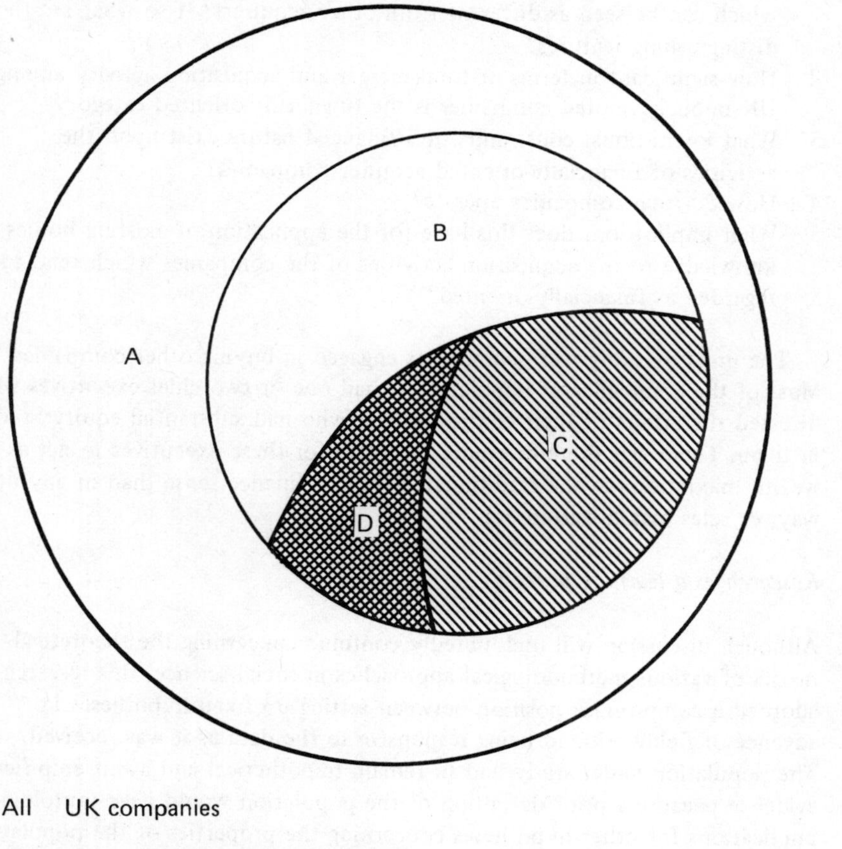

A All UK companies

B All UK publicly quoted companies

C All UK publicly quoted companies engaged in mergers and acquisitions with other UK publicly quoted companies

D A subset of C which contains acquisitions made by the hypothesized 'financially oriented' acquirer companies

Research Objectives

The research objectives were modest in terms of theoretical contribution, being rather more concerned with trying to produce a model which related to a smaller part of the whole range of mergers and acquisitions. At a later time it may prove possible to use such understanding within a more general explanatory framework for the range of mergers and acquisitions. For this reason and because of the changing economic and political environment surrounding acquisitions the contextual framework of the models was considered important. In essence the questions posed in the research were:

1 Is there a category of acquirer companies, defined as 'financially-oriented', which can be seen as different from other acquirers? If so what are their distinguishing features?
2 How significant in terms of total merger and acquisition activity amongst UK publicly quoted companies is the financially-oriented category?
3 What institutional constraints of a financial nature exist upon the activities of financially-oriented acquirer companies?
4 How do such companies operate?
5 What implications does this have for the application of existing bodies of knowledge to the acquisition activities of the companies which tend to be regarded as financially-oriented?

The units of study were companies engaged in buying other companies. Most of the companies of population D had one or two chief executives who directed the affairs of their companies and who had substantial equity holdings in them. There was therefore more incentive for these executives to act as wealth maximizers in the traditional theory of finance sense than in any other way, eg sales maximization etc.

Research as a learning process

Although discussion will undoubtedly continue concerning the theoretical merits of various methodological approaches in social science, this research adopted a compromise position between setting up fixed hypotheses in advance of fieldwork and being responsive to the data as it was received. The population under study had to remain hypothetical and await empirical evidence because a prior definition of the population would have tautological implications for other hypotheses concerning the properties of the population companies. The research proceeded in an iterative manner in the following steps:

1 Literature survey – academic, managerial texts and press cuttings.
2 Preliminary intensive interviews to gain information on population C and on the likelihood of there existing a population D.

3 Creation of an initial model (Model 1) which was a hypothetical statement of acquisition behaviour by companies in the hypothetical population D.
4 Gathering of empirical evidence for testing the existence of population D and for testing the hypotheses and assumptions of Model 1.
5 Analysis and evaluation of Model 1 in the light of the empirical data.
6 Refinement of Model 1 into Model 2 and discussion of Model 2 in terms of the existing literature concerning mergers and acquisitions.

The content of the preliminary interviews was established by reference to topics in the literature and current press cuttings. Following these interviews the research might be regarded as phases of interaction between concepts, defined in terms of hypotheses and assumptions, and empirical data which was both qualitative and quantitative. The hypotheses and assumptions were formed after the initial exposure to the practice of acquisitions by way of preliminary interviews. The research design for gathering empirical evidence in steps 2 and 4 was not closed, in other words data received other than that requested was not rejected as being of potential relevance to the research. It was found that such data had a useful role in drawing attention to areas where initial preconceptions and orientations were inappropriate. Indeed some of the richness and cohesion of the ultimate results would have been missed if data had been disregarded where it failed to relate to predetermined questions and topics.

Categories of data sought in relation to hypotheses and assumptions of model

Figures 5:4, 5:5 and 5:6 illustrate essentially quantitative components of the overall model shown in Figures 5:1 and 5:2. On the other hand the receipt of proposals for acquisition, the use of lists of acquisition proposals, and the formation of acquisition criteria were not quantitative concepts but rather summaries of behaviour patterns and information-manipulating procedures concerning which empirical evidence was sought. Although the emphasis of the research was upon the quantitative financial institutional constraints implied by the ratios Y_1 to Y_5 these more qualitative aspects were regarded as of contextual importance. Whereas the quantitative aspects of Figures 5:5 and 5:6 were hypothesized in functional mathematical forms as a set of mathematical constraints incorporating published financial data, the qualitative connective relationships were specified in a manner similar to Figures 5:1 and 5:2. Whilst it was not proposed to research the complex behavioural processes implied by each 'box' in depth, some indications as to the relevance of each box topic and of its connections to other boxes were desired. Therefore the problem arose of how to gather an appropriate mix of qualitative and quan quantitative empirical data with which to confront Model 1 and its components (although the diagrams of Figures 5:1 to 5:6 relate to Model 2, the variables and concepts are not greatly dissimilar to those of Model 1 which provided the hypothetical basis for data gathering). In addition the more macro-economic contextual questions raised by questions 1 and 2 of the research required data for empirical testing.

An early priority was to find a means of investigating question 1 above since the bulk of the research was concerned with population D which remained hypothetical until question 1 had been resolved. Preliminary interviews had shown that 'experts' in acquisition practice (acquirer company executives, merchant bankers, financial journalists, stockbrokers and investment managers) appeared to regard financially-oriented acquisitions, especially asset-stripping, as a somewhat separate activity from more 'industrially-oriented' types of acquisition. It was therefore decided to return to such experts, selected purposively, and therefore not randomly, by recommendation from contacts in the 'city', and ask them in interviews to indicate distinguishing features of financially-oriented acquirers and which companies they would place in such a category. The research process went to some length to build up to this categorization question in the questionnaire to which subsequent reference is made; fuller details can be obtained from Appendix 1 of Bean (1973). Thus the categorization of population D was established empirically over classification by the experts who were interviewed and in fact with considerable agreement, in the opinion of the author – interested readers may refer to Appendix 5 of Bean (1973). Population D is shown in Appendix 2.

In addition to this classificatory data it was necessary to obtain various types of data in response to questions 2 – 5 of the research. Question 2, which unlike the remainder of the research was tested at a macro-economic level, was investigated by collecting and analysing quantitative data concerning the quarterly number and value of bids made by companies in population C and D over a three and a half year period for which results are detailed in Chapter 3. (This data also provided some quantitative insights which helped to assess at a macro-level the change in composition of offer packages over a period of time, in particular having regard to stock market conditions.) Considerable thought was given to the most suitable means of testing the hypotheses and assumptions of Model 1 with a view to shedding light on questions 3 – 5. Statistical tests were formulated to investigate parts of Model 1 using reported accounting information to be collected from a sample of companies in population D. Ultimately these tests were rejected as a suitable research procedure in favour of a mix of interview data gathered from experts, as defined above, coupled with detailed case studies of the sequence of acquisitions by three active acquirer companies. This decision reflected worries about using accounting data alone, the desire to obtain the views of experts in the practice of acquisitions, protection against the possibility that preconceived ideas of the researcher might cause some of the most important influences to be missed in the absence of interviews with experts, and the thought that purposefully selected case studies might produce more useful data both contextual and specific to the cases. It was recognized that case study analysis alone cannot readily test general hypotheses regarding a population but each case study of an acquirer yielded a number of acquisitions, thereby providing time series data important to the models under test, and the case study data was employed in conjunction with interview data for the purposes of making any generalizations concerning population D. The case studies yielded quantitative accounting data for analysis concerning the hypothesized financial market constraints Y_1 to Y_5 and a richness of other qualitative data which would not have come from a statistical analysis. The selection of the case study companies was made by requesting an expert, with whom a good understanding of the research had been built up, to select contrasting companies within population D which would give extensive illustration of the phenomena under study. This selection process was clearly not random but nevertheless contrived to avoid some bias that might have occurred from alternative selection by the researcher whilst retaining the need for extensive information-gathering from the acquirer company case studies.

Research constraints and their effects: interview questionnaire design

The research was for a PhD dissertation and was therefore constrained by time (approximately one and a half man-years of work on the dissertation) and finance (research expenses – mainly travel – to come from doctoral programme funding). These constraints naturally exhibited themselves in the quantity of empirical data gathering and analysis which was feasible given the time required for model-building and subsequent writing-up. A further constraint was encountered in the time which experts were prepared to give for interviews. Most experts were prepared to meet for two sessions of about one hour each, the first being a preliminary interview (step 2 outlined earlier) and the second being for the main interview aided by a questionnaire (step 4). Not all interviewees were seen twice. Some of those seen at the preliminary stage were not suitable for second interviews (eg lawyers and tax consultants); therefore additional experts were recruited for step 4 alone. Three of the 24 preliminary interviewees refused a second meeting for various reasons. It was a deliberate policy to retain a flexible research stategy so that return could be made to useful sources of data to check results.

The questionnaire was employed primarily as an interview guide. Although in form it had a fairly rigid structure, in content and use it provided a means of collecting both 'yes/no/don't know' types of response and peripheral comments which proved to be extremely valuable. Frequently it was not possible to complete the questionnaire in the allotted time but this was anticipated and questions were regarded as priority or non-priority for the given type of intervieweee so that each interview time was used most productively. For example, questions about accounting for acquisitions were non-priority questions for acquirer company executives; post-acquisition capital structure change was a low-priority topic for merchant bankers. Questions were designed on a cascade basis so that one section followed through the logic of the interviewee's response to previous sections. Quite frequently questions did not need to be asked directly as respondents tended to answer them in general discussion.

Integration of qualitative and quantitative data in analysis and refinement of Model 1

The research procedures generated data from three sources: macro-quantitative data regarding value and number of bids, particularly in relation to Stock Exchange price movements, interview data primarily of a qualitative nature, and case study material which provided both qualitative and quantitative data. The macro-data had a purpose separate from the other data sources, but the interview and case study data were designed to investigate similar questions and therefore required a framework of analysis which would use both sources of data to confront the hypotheses of Model 1. The two sources of data were independently derived and therefore it was decided to analyse Model 1 against each source of data separately so that their independence could be used to good advantage; a third analysis section was then devoted to discussion of the results of these two data sets together in respect of the various hypotheses.

The character of the interview data is worth brief comment. The questions were in some cases of the 'yes/no/don't know' variety for which responses and consequent analysis were straightforward. More frequently respondents tended to elaborate on questionnaire topics and thereby provided a considerable amount of further contextual data which yielded valuable perspectives concerning the reasons for variations in responses amongst those interviewed. However these comments raised problems in analysing the data. The following extracts are examples of summarized comments which were relevant to testing parts of Model 1.

> With respect to sources of acquisition proposals,
>
> One acquirer company executive:
>
> > I take a fistful of Extel cards home on the train each night.
>
> Three other acquirer company executives:
>
> > Merger brokers produce quite a lot of suggestions but they are generally not very useful.
>
> With regard to the combination of equity, loans and cash instruments in an offer package,
>
> Three merchant bankers and one financial journalist:
>
> > One can issue less popular stocks as acquisition instruments because of the captive market, ie the target company shareholders. This gives scope for some quite sharp deals and the ability to 'ram unpopular paper down the throats of seller shareholders'. No prospectus is needed for acquisition instruments.
>
> Three acquirer company executives:
>
> > Although there may be apparent immediate dilution in earnings per share as a result of an acquisition and the financing package employed, one can pull the acquisition round sufficiently quickly so that no dilution occurs when the acquirer's annual results come out. ('One can wash its face in the first six months.')

To coerce such data into categories would have lost much of the richness of the responses; instead it was decided to first retain the comments in their original form and classify them by topics which related directly to the hypotheses and assumptions of Model 1 and then to try to summarize similar comments by different interview respondents into the form of those illustrated above. In this way the total interview data base was brought down to approximately 250 summarized comments, each being the result of actual comments by between one and 18 interview respondents. This method preserved much of the contextual richness of the individual replies yet proved manageable for analytic and reference purposes. The hypotheses and assumptions of Model 1 were then analysed in the light of the summarized comments which were further classified as 'favourable', 'unfavourable' or 'neutral' to Model 1; the results of this analysis were a general discussion and a set of condensed statements labelled 'contentions' about aspects of Model 1 as a result of testing against this interview data. For example one contention was:

> Earnings per share growth alone is not the operational goal of financially-oriented acquirers. Instead the operational translation of shareholder net present wealth maximization is a balance between growth in assets and earnings per share over a time horizon of up to two years ahead.

These contentions, of which there were 25 arising from the mainly qualitative interview data, formed a means of reference for the phase of integrating the interview results with the mainly quantitative case study results. In fact the case studies produced quantitative data on 21 of the 25 contentions so that most of the hypotheses and assumptions of Model 1 received testing from both sources of data.

The case studies yielded sufficient quantitative data to enable quantitative tests to be carried out on aspects of Model 1 which resulted in Figures 5:5 and 5:6 illustrated earlier. (This again is a judgment of the researcher's; interested readers can refer to Bean (1973), especially Chapter 5 and Appendices 8, 9 and 10.) For example the impact of financial market constraints was investigated by reference to the constraint levels implied by the public company bids made by the case study acquirer companies. Specifically the constraint values were calculated and the financial packages used in the bids were compared with the solutions which would have been obtained by a linear-programming method along the lines proposed by Figure 5:6 using the constraint limits reported in the interview data; in almost all cases the results were complementary. The concept of financial market constraints and interview comments suggested how bid premiums might be formed and it was possible to test these ideas using quantitative data from the case studies. Chapter 4 details these results. Further areas where the case study data provided insights of a quantitative nature which could be used in conjunction with the interview results included:

Acquisition cash payback periods – see Chapter 3
An index constructed to show the 'quality of a deal' in terms of increments to the acquirer company's assets and earnings per share – see Chapter 3.
The effects of share incentive schemes and personal equity holdings upon directors' wealth deriving from salaries and shareholdings respectively – see Chapter 3.
Frequency of acquisition deals – see Chapter 3.
The effects of financial market operations in target company shares upon bid premiums – see Chapter 4.
Convertible loan terms – see Chapter 4.

Concluding comments: research procedure and data integration

Preliminary interviews and familiarization with the subject matter prior to constructing Model 1 was an essential stage in the research. Without it the remainder of the work would have lacked focus and the hypotheses and assumptions of Model 1 could not have been stated so clearly; this would in turn have had damaging effects on construction of the interview questionnaire. In spite of this familiarization with the research area prior to the main data gathering, fresh ideas and unexpected behaviour patterns of varying importance to the research came to light during the main data gathering phase.

A flexible interview approach was an advantage. If too structured a questionnaire had been rigidly followed during interviews much useful data would have been missed which was particularly relevant in yielding perspectives upon qualitative relationships amongst topics in the hypothetical models.

The availability of interview respondents and the quality of their responses naturally varied, so interview structure and data gathering had to anticipate variable extent and quality of responses. It proved quite easy to obtain two sessions of approximately one hour each from top executives in the subject area and most of them were prepared to talk frankly about their activities. This may have reflected the fact that most of the organizations studied were young, successful and largely equated with their top executives.

The research employed interview and case study material, the former being mainly qualitative and the latter mainly quantitative. The interview material and the peripheral comments associated with responses supported ideas expressed in other reports of sociological enquiries that it is often inappropriate to take data out of its context simply to coerce it into numerical categories for quantitative analysis; much sensitivity can be lost in the process.

Whilst case study results alone cannot justifiably be used in generalizations, in conjunction with results from other data sources they can more justifiably serve such purposes. In addition case study data at one level of generalization can yield statistical data at another; for example each case study yielded data for a number of individual acquisitions. The case studies' quantitative data input gave insights into functional relationships such as those illustrated in Figures 5:5 and 5:6 which interview data could not; however, the latter yielded most of the data concerning the qualitative relationships, such as those shown in Figure 5:2. The case studies also helped to clarify relationships amongst qualitative aspects of the models, especially components of the screening processes shown in Figure 5:2 and the extent to which time sequences of acquisitions were compatible with changing constraints as a result of previous acquisitions.

Unexpected leads which implied changes in preconceptions of the researcher arose from both interview and case study data sources. It was usually possible to check such leads against data from the other source as a means of assessing its relevance to the hypotheses and assumptions of Model 1. This would not have been possible if the research design had not been structured before data gathering to obtain data from both interview and case study sources in response of similar questions, ie the hypotheses and assumptions of Model 1.

Bibliography

Aguilar F.J., *Scanning the Business Environment*, Collier-Macmillan, London, 1967

Alberts W.W. and Segall J.E., Eds., *The Corporate Merger*, University of Chicago Press, Chicago and London, 1966

Altman E.I., 'Financial Ratios, Discriminant Analysis and the Prediction of Corporate Bankruptcy', *Journal of Finance*, September 1968, pp. 589-609.

Ansoff H.I., *Corporate Strategy*, Penguin Book, London, 1968

Baumol W.J., 'On the Theory of Expansion of the Firm', *American Economic Review*, December 1962, pp. 1078-87

Baumol W.J., Malkiel B.G. and Quandt R.E., 'The Valuation of Convertible Securities', *Quarterly Journal of Economics*, February 1966, pp. 48-59

Baumol W.J. and Quandt R.E., 'Investment and Discount Rates under Capital Rationing – a Programming Approach', *Economic Journal*, June 1965, pp. 317-29

Bean D.G., 'Financial Strategy in Acquisition Decisions', unpublished Doctoral Thesis, Manchester Business School, University of Manchester, 1973

Beer S., *Brain of the Firm – the Managerial Cybernetics of Organization*, Allen Lane, The Penguin Press, London, 1972

Black F. and Scholes M., 'The Pricing of Options and Corporate Liabilities', *Journal of Political Economy*, May/June 1973, pp. 637-54

Blume M.E., 'Portfolio Theory: a Step towards its Practical Application', *Journal of Business*, April 1970, pp. 152-73

Bodenhorn D., 'A Cash-flow Concept of Profit', *Journal of Finance*, March 1964, pp. 16-31

Carleton W.T., 'Linear Programming and Capital Budgeting Models: a New Interpretation', *Journal of Finance*, December 1969, pp. 825-33

Chambers D., 'Programming the Allocation of Funds subject to Restrictions on Reported Results', *Operations Research Quarterly*, December 1967, pp. 407-32.

Chesham Research Unit, 'Attitudes of Private Shareholders to Mergers and Acquisitions', Chesham Occasional Paper No. 5, London, 1971

Clarkson G.P.E., *Portfolio Selection: A Simulation of Trust Investment*, Prentice-Hall, Englewood Cliffs, New Jersey, 1962

Cyert R.M. and March J.G., *A Behavioural Theory of the Firm*, Prentice-Hall, Englewood Cliffs, New Jersey, 1963

Fama E.F., 'Efficient Capital Markets: a Review of Theory and Empirical Work', *Journal of Finance*, May 1970, pp. 383-423

Fama E.F., 'Portfolio Analysis in a Stable Paretian Market', *Management Science*, January 1965, pp. 404-19

Fama E.F., Fisher L., Jensen M.C. and Roll R., 'The Adjustment of Stock Prices to New Information', *International Economic Review*, February 1969, pp. 1-21

Fama E.F. and Roll R., 'Some Properties of Symmetric Stable Distributions', *American Statistical Association Journal*, September 1968, pp. 817-36

Fama E.F. and Roll R., 'Parameter Estimates for Symmetric Stable Distributions', *American Statistical Association Journal*, June 1971, pp. 331-8

Farrar D.E., *The Investment Decision Under Uncertainty*, Markham, Chicago, 1967

Forrester J.W., *Industrial Dynamics*, MIT Press, Cambridge, Massachusetts, 1961

Friend I. and Puckett M., 'Dividends and Stock Prices', *American Economic Review*, September 1964, pp. 657-82.

Gordon M.J., 'Towards a Theory of Financial Distress', *Journal of Finance*, May 1971, pp. 347-57

Granger C.W.J. and Morgenstern O., *Predictability of Stock Market Prices*, D.C. Heath, Lexington, Massachusetts, 1970

Haynes W.W. and Solomon M.B., 'A Misplaced Emphasis in Capital Budgeting', *Quarterly Review of Economics and Business*, February 1962, pp. 39-46

Hertz D.B., 'Risk Analysis in Capital Investment', *Harvard Business Review*, January-February 1964, pp. 95-106

Jensen M.C., 'Risk, the Pricing of Capital Assets, and the Evaluation of Investment Portfolios', *Journal of Business*, April 1969, pp. 167-247

Kitching J., 'Why do Mergers Miscarry?', *Harvard Business Review*, November-December 1967, pp. 84-101

Kuehn D.A., 'Stock Market Valuation and Acquisitions: an Empirical Test of One Component of Managerial Utility', *Journal of Industrial Economics*, 1968-9, pp. 132-45

Lawson G.H. and Bean D.G., *Enterprise Valuation; A Cash Flow Approach*, commissioned by Union Européenne des Experts Comptable Economiques et Financiers (UEC)

Levy H. and Sarnat M., 'Diversification, Portfolio Analysis and the Uneasy Case for Conglomerate Mergers', *Journal of Finance*, September 1970, pp. 795-803

Linowes D.F., 'Managing Growth Through Acquisition', American Management Association, 1968

Lintner J., 'Dividends, Earnings, Leverage, Stock Prices and the Supply of Capital to Corporations', *Review of Economics and Statistics*, August 1962, pp. 243-69

Lintner J., 'The Cost of Capital and Optimal Financing of Corporate Growth', *Journal of Finance*, May 1963, pp. 292-310

Lintner J., 'Optimal Dividends and Corporate Growth Under Uncertainty', *Quarterly Journal of Economics*, February 1964, pp. 49-95

Lintner J., 'The Valuation of Risk Assets and the Selection of Risky Investments in Stock Portfolios and Capital Budgets', *Review of Economics and Statistics*, February 1965, pp. 13-37

Lupton T. and Wilson C.S., 'The Social Background and Connections of Top Decisions Makers', *Manchester School*, January 1959, pp. 30-51

Mackintosh A.S., *The Development of the Firm*, Cambridge University Press, Cambridge, 1963

Mandelbrot B., 'The Variation of Certain Speculative Prices', *Journal of Business*, October 1963, pp. 393-413

Mandelbrot B., 'Forecasts of Future Prices, Unbiased Markets and "Martingale" Models', *Journal of Business*, January 1966, pp. 242-55

Mandelbrot B., 'The Variation of Some Other Speculative Prices', *Journal of Business*, October 1967, pp. 393-413

Mandelbrot,B., 'Long-Run Linearity, Locally Gaussian Process, H-Spectra and Infinite Variances', *International Economic Review*, February 1969, pp. 82-111

Markowitz H.M., *Portfolio Selection*, John Wiley, New York, 1959

Marris R., *The Economic Theory of 'Managerial' Capitalism*, Macmillan, London, 1966

Merrett A.J. and Sykes A., *The Finance and Analysis of Capital Projects*, Longmans Green, London, 1963

Merton R.C., 'Theory of Rational Option Pricing', *Bell Journal of Economics and Management Science*, Spring 1973, pp. 141-75

Modigliani F and Miller M.H., 'The Cost of Capital, Corporation Finance and the Theory of Investment', *American Economic Review*, June 1958, pp. 261-97

Modigliani F. and Miller M.H., 'Corporate Income Taxes and the Cost of Capital: a Correction', *American Economic Review*, June 1963, pp. 433-43

Modigliani F. and Miller M.H., 'Some Estimates of the Cost of Capital to the Electric Utility Industry, 1954-57', *American Economic Review*, June 1966, pp. 333-91

Mossin J., 'Merger Agreements: some Game-Theoretic Considerations', *Journal of Business*, October 1968, pp. 460-71

Narver J.C., *Conglomerate Mergers and Market Competition*, University of California Press, Berkeley and Los Angeles, 1967

Newbould G.D., *Management and Merger Activity*, Guthstead Ltd, Liverpool, 1970

Orcutt G.H., Greenberger M., Korbel J. and Rivlin A.M., *Microanalysis of Socioeconomic Systems: a Simulation Study*, Harper & Row, New York, 1961

Panel on Takeovers and Mergers, *The City Code on Takeovers and Mergers*, London, 1972 and 1974

Penrose E.T., *The Theory of the Growth of the Firm*, Basil Blackwell, Oxford, 1966

Rayner A.C. and Little I.M.D., *Higgledy Piggledy Growth Again*, Basil Blackwell, Oxford, 1966

Samuelson P.A., 'Proof that Properly Anticipated Prices Fluctuate Randomly', *Industrial Management Review*, Spring 1965, pp. 41-9

Sharpe W.F., 'Capital Asset Prices: a Theory of Market Equilibrium under Conditions of Risk', *Journal of Finance*, September 1964, pp. 425-42

Silberman I.H., 'A Note on Merger Valuation', *Journal of Finance*, June 1968, pp. 528-36

Simon H.A., 'A Behavioural Model of Rational Choice', *Quarterly Journal of Economics*, February 1955, pp. 99-118

Simon H.A., 'On the Concept of Organizational Goal', *Administrative Science Quarterly*, March 1964, pp. 1-22

Singh A. and Whittington G., *Growth, Profitability and Valuation*, Cambridge University Press, Cambridge, 1968

Solomon E., *The Theory of Financial Management*, Columbia University Press, New York and London, 1963

Stapleton R.C., 'Merger Bargaining and Financial Strategy', *Manchester School*, August 1971, pp. 131-44

Taylor F.W., 'Anatomy of a Merger', *Mergers and Acquisitions*, November-December 1970, pp. 1-9

Vance J.O., 'Is Your Company a Takeover Target?', *Harvard Business Review*, May-June 1969, pp. 93-8

Weinberg M.A., *Takeovers and Amalgamations*, Sweet & Maxwell, London, 1971

Weston J.F., 'Reply to Silberman's "A Note on Merger Valuation"', *Journal of Finance*, June 1968, pp. 528-36

Williamson O.E., *The Economics of Discretionary Behaviour – Managerial Objectives in a Theory of the Firm*, Markham Publishing Company, Chicago, 1967

Wyatt A.R. and Kieso D.E., *Business Combinations: Planning and Action*, International Textbook Company, Pennsylvania, 1969

Index

Certain references in this index may only lead to footnote indices: users unable to find the name or subject matter on the page indicated should turn to the notes at the end of the chapter for the necessary guidance.